Leadership
in the
Church

Leadership
in the
Church

HOW THE TRADITIONAL ROLES CAN SERVE
THE CHRISTIAN COMMUNITY TODAY

Walter Cardinal Kasper

Translated by Brian McNeil

A Herder & Herder Book
The Crossroad Publishing Company
New York

The Crossroad Publishing Company
www.crossroadpublishing.com

Copyright © 2003 by the Crossroad Publishing Company

All rights reserved. No part of this book may be reproduced, stored in a retrieval system, or transmitted, in any form or by any means, electronic, mechanical, photocopying, recording, or otherwise, without the written permission of The Crossroad Publishing Company.

Printed in the United States of America

This book is set in 12/17 Centaur.
The display type is Bodoni Antiqua,

Library of Congress Cataloging-in-Publication Data

Kasper, Walter, 1933-
   [Essays. English. Selections]
   Leadership in the Church : how the traditional roles can serve the Christian community today / Walter Kasper ; translated by Brian McNeil.
      p.   cm.
   "A Herder & Herder book."
   Includes bibliographical references.
   ISBN **978-0-8245-9964-5**(alk. paper)
   1. Church. 2. Catholic Church — Clergy. 3. Catholic Church — Doctrines.   I. Title.
BX1746.K345213 2002
230'.2 — dc21

                                        2002004178

Contents

Foreword   9

1. The Diaconate   13

    The Deacon's Ministry, 13 / *Communio*-Ecclesiology as the Basis of the Diaconate, 24 / Contemporary Relevance of *Communio-Diaconia*, 31 / Some Concrete Observations on the Form of the Diaconate Today, 38

2. Priestly Office   45

    Recent Discussions of the Topic, 45 / The Representative Character of the Apostolic Office, 49 / The Apostolic Office: Representation of Jesus Christ as Head of the Church, 55 / The Apostolic Ministry as Representation of the Church, 59 / The Task of Leading the Community, 64 / Collaboration by Laypersons in Tasks of Community Leadership, 68 / Concluding Perspectives, 72

3. Episcopal Office   76

    In Search of a New Vision of the Church, 76 / The Spiritual and Pastoral Character of the Episcopal Office, 83 / The Sacramental Dimension of the Episcopal Office, 96

4. The Apostolic Succession:
   An Ecumenical Problem   114

   The Problem, 114 / Biblical Foundations of the
   Apostolic Succession, 117 / Apostolic Succession in the
   Early Church as the Framework for a Future Consensus,
   122 / The Divergence of Tradition and Succession
   in the Middle Ages and in the Reformation, 127 /
   Convergences since the Second Vatican Council —
   and the Difference That Remains, 133 / The Goal:
   An Agreement to Differ on the Understanding of the
   Apostolic Succession, 138

5. Canon Law: The Normative Application
   of Justice and Mercy   144

   Mercy as the Fulfillment of Justice, 145 / Human
   Salvation: The Meaning of Canon Law, 149 / Canonical
   Equity as a Principle for the Application of Canonical
   Norms, 151 / An Ecclesial Legal Culture Inspired by
   the Gospel, 155

6. The Universal Church and the Local Church:
   A Friendly Rejoinder   158

   An Urgent Pastoral Problem, 158 / Historical Perspectives, 163 / Common Ecclesiological Presuppositions,
   167 / Controversy about a Scholastic Dispute, 169 /
   The Ecumenical Perspective, 173

7. Ecumenical Perspectives on the Future:
   One Lord, One Faith, One Baptism   176

   The Changed Situation, 176 / The Ecumenical Breakthrough, 178 / Where Are We Now?, 184 / Two Milestones along the Ecumenical Path, 187 / The Ecclesiological Question That Remains Open, 190 / A Different Understanding of the Church, 193 / A Turning Point Has Been Reached, 198 / Courage for the Ecumenical Task, 201

Notes   205

The First Publication of the Essays   239

Foreword

Walter Kasper is becoming increasingly better known to English speakers and readers. This is a positive development, for he is a distinguished theologian not only for his own Roman Catholic Church but for the wider ecumenical church. Until recently most of Kasper's theological work was pursued in the context of German academia and international ecumenism. He was for a number of years professor of dogmatic theology at the University of Tübingen. At the same time he served as a member of the Commission on Faith and Order of the World Council of Churches and of various theological dialogues. His writings, especially those on the church, sacraments, and infallibility, including his debate with his mentor Karl Rahner on infallibility, have been helpful and clarifying to people of a number of Christian traditions. Unfortunately, too little of his significant work has been translated into English. This volume helps correct this deficiency.

In 1989 Kasper became the bishop of Rottenburg-Stuttgart in the Republic of Germany, a position he held until 1999, when he was named the secretary of the Pontifical Council for Promoting Christian Unity at the Vatican. In 2001, Kasper was selected to be the president of that Pontifical Council and created a cardinal by Pope John Paul II. His career reflects the multifaceted nature of the man: a committed and faithful member of the church and a Christian thinker of extraordinary ability.

Leadership in the Church is a collection of essays previously published in German over the last several years. These essays deal with critical topics for all Christians, and certainly for those committed to the unity of Christ's church. English readers now have a set of well-translated works of Cardinal Kasper, which explore such timely and relevant topics as the diaconate, the episcopal office, apostolic succession, the universal and local church — a subject of lively encounter between Cardinals Kasper and Ratzinger — and the future of ecumenism.

Within these pages can be found some of the best contemporary Roman Catholic thought available on many of the most pressing challenges facing all the churches. Participants in theological dialogues involving the Roman Catholic Church, be they Catholic or ecumenical partners, will find fresh insights into thorny issues that require discussion and resolution within and between churches. Thoughtful readers will learn much about the current state of Christian theology. While the book is indeed erudite, it is not pedantic. It speaks about the theme of leadership and the issues confronting all Christians on the threshold of this new century.

When the invitation to write this brief foreword came, my initial reaction was: "Here is another task to be done in the midst of busy days, even though the book is authored by a person whom I have known over the years and greatly admire." Having now studied the book carefully, I can say that it is one of the most important works I have read recently. I was familiar with most of the pieces in their earlier published form, but I gained a new appreciation of their significance and contribution. I am indebted to the translator and publisher for what they have provided to a larger audience. I am sure that I will not be alone in the high regard in which I hold this work and its author.

WILLIAM G. RUSCH
Executive Director
Foundation for a Conference on
Faith and Order in North America

– 1 –

The Diaconate

The Deacon's Ministry

Even the simple observation that the diaconate is a fundamental and essential ministry in our church today is enough to provoke heated emotional debates. The diaconate is still far from being firmly rooted in the local churches. Still less can it be taken for granted, as the terminological uncertainties show. While it goes without saying that a priest is "ordained," we sometimes hear that a deacon is merely "installed," and Masses in which laypersons are commissioned for ecclesial service often seem indistinguishable from an ordination ceremony. More than thirty years have passed since the Second Vatican Council, but much in the theological understanding of the ministry of the diaconate remains unclear and a matter of theological dispute, resulting in the variety of pastoral tasks assigned to deacons.

It is well known that very different motives led the council fathers to take up the idea of a renewal of the permanent diaconate. Some foresaw the future shortage of priests and hoped that permanent deacons would relieve the pressure on the clergy in face of the increasing diaspora in the older dioceses and the missionary situation in the younger local churches.[1] For others, the starting point was the diaconal groups that had come into existence even before the council: these bishops hoped for an invigoration of the church's *diaconia*.[2] Still others saw the obligation to celibacy, and indeed the whole question of celibacy, as the basic issue involved in the introduction of the permanent diaconate.[3]

The question of celibacy was particularly important to those who opposed the permanent diaconate, since they feared a debate about priestly celibacy. In this essay, I shall leave this question aside, as well as the issue of the ordination of women to the diaconate; such problems require a separate discussion. My point of departure is the assumption that the shortage of priests is not the key to our understanding of the deacon, whose ministry was envisaged by the council as an autonomous grade of the sacrament of orders: deacons are not substitutes to be brought in where priests are lacking. I wish to pursue the second idea mentioned above, since I believe that the perspective of *diaconia* can indicate the path that deacons should take in the future.

Reflection on pastoral concerns and experiences had paved the way for the introduction of the permanent diaconate in many dioceses throughout the world; it was the fruit of a movement "from below," especially the so-called diaconal groups, which had been encouraged by Pope Pius XII and were discussed by many bishops at the Second Vatican Council. In keeping with these ideas, conciliar discussions concentrated on the pragmatic pastoral aspects of the diaconate rather than on its theological elements. Nevertheless, fundamental theological reflections by Karl Rahner, Yves Congar, and others soon established clearly that the diaconate was not one particular form of the lay apostolate, but was a special articulation of the ordained ministry in the church. This view was confirmed by the council, and has since found universal acceptance.

The council sees the diaconate as "a ministry vitally necessary to the life of the church." It explicitly affirms that it intends to facilitate the introduction of the permanent diaconate because it would otherwise be difficult to ensure the exercise of those tasks that belong to the theological essence of the diaconal ministry.[4]

The foundations of the theology of ecclesial ministry are formulated in a binding manner in *Lumen Gentium*, the constitution on the church, which declares that both diaconate and presbyterate belong to the one sacramental ordained ministry, which is conferred by the laying on of hands and prayer, and which is exercised in its fullness by the episcopate.[5] Even a slight acquaintance with church history will remind us that such an affirmation was no mere commonplace at the time of the council: it goes behind the medieval development to take up anew the liturgy and theology of the first centuries. More precisely, it breaks with the medieval restriction of church ministry to the priestly office, which was understood exclusively on the basis of the priest's power to consecrate the Eucharist — for such a view made it impossible to understand either episcopal or diaconal ordination as a sacrament.

This renewal was made possible by recourse to the ordination liturgies of the early church and the theology of the patristic period. In the light of this older tradition, the council was able to teach solemnly that diaconate, presbyterate, and episcopate belong to the *one* sacramental ministry of the church. Accordingly, the repristination of the diaconate as a sacramental ecclesial office was the fruit both of a pastoral reflection on present-day needs and of a theological reflection on the authoritative sources of the church's faith. Only this double movement allowed the renewal of the diaconate to take a binding form in the church.

The council also brought about an important change in the understanding of the relationships between episcopate, presbyterate, and diaconate. Until the Second Vatican Council, the various grades of ordination could be understood as an ascending *cursus*. The council reversed the order of perception when it followed the early church in beginning with the bishop, as the one who has the fullness of the sacrament of orders.[6] Deacons and priests have each their own specific gradated participation in the one sacramental office that the bishop possesses in fullness; the council sees them as collaborators of the bishop, dependent on him and subordinate to him. Their ministry is to represent the bishop, who needs collaborators and helpers because of the sheer volume of work that is expected of him.

Subordination to the bishop does not, of course, make deacons merely his private servants. The sacrament of ordination is conferred by Jesus Christ himself and imprints a sacramental character (*character indelebilis*) on the one ordained, conforming him in a special manner to Christ, who is the one high priest, pastor, and bishop. Hence, the bishop does not have full authority over either the ordination itself or the ordinand: the sacrament of orders gives the ordinand an immediate relationship to Christ, which entails a certain autonomy and responsibility that the bishop must respect. Bishops, priests, and deacons share, each in their own way, in the one mission of Jesus Christ, and they must collaborate in a fraternal and collegial manner. Priests and deacons are no mere subjects of the bishop: he must address them and treat them as brothers and friends.

The varied participation in the one ministry of Jesus Christ has consequences for the way we define the relationship between the priestly and the diaconal ministries. As long as the diaconate was only an intermediate stage en route to the priesthood, it seemed obvious that the deacon was subordinate to the priest in the hierarchical structure. At first sight, *Lumen Gentium* 29 appears to retain this language of hierarchical subordination: "At a lower level of the hierarchy are to be found deacons...." Closer examination of the text reveals, however, that it is not speaking of a subordination of the deacon to the priest, but of a lesser participation by the deacon in the bishop's ministry. This can be seen perfectly clearly in *Lumen Gentium* 28, where we read: "Christ, whom the Father hallowed and sent into the world (John 10:36), has, through his apostles, made their successors, the bishops namely, sharers in his consecration and mission; and these, in their turn, duly entrusted in varying degrees various members of the church with the office of their ministry. Thus the divinely instituted ecclesiastical ministry is exercised in different degrees by those who even from ancient times have been called bishops, priests, and deacons." The gradations in participation in the bishop's ministry thus denote two different structures: the bishop is aided by two separate arms (so to speak), which have differing tasks but must collaborate with one another.

This conciliar text "means the abandonment of the traditional theology of the sacrament of orders, which envisaged an ascending *cursus* of ordinations and understood episcopal ordination as a nonessential addition to priestly ordination."[7] Our theology now must see ordination as imparting a differentiated share in the episcopal ministry. This means that deacons are immediately subordinate to the bishop; naturally, this entails fraternal collaboration with the priests who likewise share in his ministry.

The Second Vatican Council agrees here with the perspective of the first centuries. Paul mentions the deacons in immediate connection with the *episkopoi* (Phil. 1:1), and Ignatius of Antioch calls them the *sundouloi* ("fellow slaves") of the bishop (i.e., not of the priests).[8] According to the *Apostolic Tradition* of Hippolytus, deacons are ordained "not for the priesthood, but for the service of the bishop, to carry out the tasks he gives them."[9] The *Didascalia Apostolorum* exhorts: "Be of one mind, you bishops and deacons, for you form one single body." The deacon is called "the bishop's ear, mouth, heart and soul."[10] At certain periods, as Jerome and Ambrosiaster relate, deacons seem to have occupied positions of such power at the bishop's right hand that the priests were moved to vigorous protest. After this clarification about the participation of the diaconate in the one ordained sacramental ministry of the church, we must now look more closely at the specific substance that this one ministry assumes in the office of deacon.

The decisive point is made in *Lumen Gentium* with the help of an abbreviated quotation from the *Apostolic Tradition* of Hippolytus. The council makes a clear distinction between priestly and diaconal ministries when it emphasizes that the deacon is ordained "not for the priesthood, but for service [*ministerium*]." The deacon is not a "mini-priest" who fills gaps left where no priests are available, nor is his ministry a mere transitional stage on the path to the priesthood. It is an autonomous ministry, a specific articulation of the ministerial service entrusted to the church by Jesus Christ.

Ordination "for service" means that the deacon is charged in a special way with the Christian *diaconia*. We read already in the Acts of the Apostles that the apostles were unable to perform the ministry of the tables alone and needed helpers if they were not to abandon the ministry of the Word (6:2). Ignatius of Antioch writes that the deacons are entrusted with the ministry of Jesus Christ,[11] and the church order of Hippolytus says that they are to care for the sick and to inform the bishop about them.[12] In the early church, bishops often gave the deacons the task of caring for the poor. The council explicitly quotes Polycarp's exhortation that deacons should be "merciful, zealous, walking according to the truth of the Lord who became the servant of all."[13]

It is, of course, perfectly true that baptism and confirmation obligate *all* Christians to love their neighbor and serve their brothers and sisters, and that (as the Second Vatican Council unceasingly emphasizes) *all* who hold office in the church are called to service. This applies to the office of priest and of bishop, as *Lumen Gentium* 24 states with particular clarity: "That office... is, in the strict sense of the term, a service, which is called very expressively in Sacred Scripture a *diaconia*, or ministry (see Acts 1:17, 25; 21:10; Rom. 11:13; 1 Tim. 1:12)." It is, therefore, the common task of bishops, priests, and deacons to exercise the *diakonia* of Jesus Christ in his name vis-à-vis all who are poor or suffer in any way, and to promote this work in the church; the deacon has a particular share in this diaconal task of the bishop. "In a special manner, he is to represent the specifically diaconal dimension of all church ministry, i.e., the servant-ministry of Jesus Christ in the church."[14]

This diaconal ministry of the deacon is not a one-sided social or charitable task: deacons are not ordained social workers! Ignatius of Antioch calls them "deacons of the mysteries of Jesus Christ," echoing 1 Cor. 4:1, "for they are not deacons in view of food and drink, but servants of the church of God."[15] They are "more closely bound to the altar"[16] and share in the ministry of preaching.[17] Accordingly, the *diaconia* that the deacon exercises in the name of Jesus Christ must be understood in a comprehensive theological and ecclesiological sense as including the ministry of proclamation and service in the altar, as well as leadership tasks.[18]

There are, in fact, not only the materially poor; there are also those starving intellectually and spiritually, and all too often they are left alone in their searching. Therefore, evangelizing too is a service to others. Teaching the ignorant has always counted as one of the spiritual works of mercy, and a widespread lack of orientation makes this all the more important today. Likewise, bringing the eucharistic gifts from the altar to the sick and the dying — one of the fundamental tasks of the deacon from the very beginning — has always been seen as a work of Christian *diaconia*. Finally, it is a work of love and mercy to visit lonely persons and bring them together with others, thus building up the Christian community. When we speak of the ministry of the deacon from the perspective of *diaconia*, we must include all three basic dimensions of ecclesial ministry, namely, *martyria* and *liturgia* as well as *diaconia* in the narrower sense of the word.

H. Hoping puts this point as follows:

> Priests represent the bishop locally, i.e., in the parishes, by bearing the ultimate responsibility for leading the communities to which they are assigned. This is why they also preside at the celebration of the Eucharist. In this sense, they have a large share in the apostolic mission of the bishop. Deacons too share in this apostolic mission, but

they represent the bishop locally in the *diaconia*...for which he is responsible as church leader. As a task incumbent upon the ministry of church leadership, this *diaconia* must be distinguished from the active love of neighbor (*caritas*), which faith inspires in every Christian, just as it must be distinguished from the structured "diaconal" work carried out in Protestant and Catholic charitable organizations. Since the priest represents the bishop locally, the deacon cannot be unrelated to him: this is why *Lumen Gentium* 29 says that deacons should exercise their ministry "in fellowship with the bishop and his presbyterate." If one of the fundamental functions of ecclesial office is to represent the service of Christ, the head and Lord of the church, then this applies also to the diaconate, which belongs to the ecclesial *ordo*. Accordingly, in the Catholic understanding, deacons have a share in the authority which leads the church.[19]

To sum up: the deacon represents in a particular manner Jesus Christ, who came in order to serve (Mark 10:45) and humbled himself to take on the form of a slave (Phil. 2:7f.). As the bishop's local representative, the deacon leads (i.e., inspires and motivates) the *diacona* of the community, in collaboration with the priests. Hence, thanks to the share in ministry that they receive in view of *diaconia*, the deacons also share in the authority of church leadership. As an ordained ministry, the diaconate makes it clear that *diaconia* is an essential dimension of the responsibility for leading the church.

After this clarification of the special ministry of the deacon, we must now ask where it fits into the conciliar ecclesiology as a whole and how it is related to the *communio*-ecclesiology of the council, which took up one of the most urgent questions of our time, namely, the yearning for fellowship, and helped many Christians to realize that "we all are church." Why do we need deacons in our church today?

Communio-Ecclesiology as the Basis of the Diaconate

Jesus Christ gave us the Lord's Prayer, the beautiful prayer that allows us to affirm and confess that we all have one common Father, and that we are his children. This is a deeply moving idea: in the presence of God, and thanks to his gift, I belong with everyone else to the one family of our common Father in heaven. This means that isolation, loneliness, alienation, and *a fortiori* enmity are signs of sin. God did not wish to save and sanctify human beings in the dispensation of salvation as single individuals independently of all their mutual relationships: God wished to make them his people. Accordingly, the council understands the church as a "messianic people" that, "although it does not actually include all persons, and at times may appear as a small flock, is, however, a most sure seed of unity, hope, and salvation for the whole human race."[20]

The *communio*-ecclesiology of the council takes up this salvation-historical view of the church. It is not only relevant to the questions that arise within the church itself: it shows where the church belongs in the total history of salvation and of the world. Ultimately, it helps give substance to the fundamental conciliar affirmation that the church is in Jesus Christ as it were the sacrament, i.e., the sign and instrument of unity,[21] and this makes it one of the most important of the council's inspirations: "For the church, there is only one path into the future, namely, the way indicated by the council. This path means that full realization of the council and of the conciliar ecclesiology of *communio*."[22] The church is seen to exist, not for its own sake but for others: for human beings, for a world in need of unity, reconciliation, and peace. The church is a servant church. In its broadest sense, then, *diaconia* is not just one dimension of the church: it is its essential dimension.

The Acts of the Apostles expresses the concrete meaning of *communio*-ecclesiology in these words: "They devoted themselves to the apostles' teaching and fellowship, to the breaking of bread and the prayers" (2:42). Here, the church is the fellowship of those who have accepted the message about Jesus, the incarnate love of God, thanks to the testimony of the apostles; they share this message, are united in this message, and remain faithful to it. The church is the fellowship of those who share in the one eucharistic bread and thus form one body (see I Cor. 10:17), since (as Augustine says) the Eucharist is the "sacrament of unity."[23] Finally, the church is the fellowship of those who realize in every sphere of life the fellowship that is founded in Jesus' praxis, revealed in his word, and celebrated in the Eucharist, as they share their daily bread and their possessions. Since *martyria, liturgia,* and *diaconia* are thus the three fundamental dimensions of the church, *diaconia* as the realization of love is the logical consequence (and the criterion of authenticity) of faith and of the Eucharist, both for every community and for each individual.

The basis of this affirmation is the message that Jesus proclaimed and his own ways of acting. His pastoral service was a ministry of salvation and healing, symbolized in the miracles he worked when confronted with various kinds of distress — feeding the hungry, healing the sick, raising the dead, driving out demons. In keeping with this, Jesus sent out his disciples, not only to preach and teach, but also to heal (Matt. 10:8). This dimension is often forgotten, but this is the reason why the church's teaching and pastoral office too must be realized in healing actions and the diaconal service of charity: it is these that demonstrate the church's credibility. As the local church, every community must ensure the realization of *diaconia*, which provides orientation for faith and preaching, for the Eucharist and the liturgy. Faith without *diaconia* is not Christian faith; preaching without *diaconia* is not Christian preaching. It is indeed true that a community that celebrates the Eucharist but is not orientated toward *diaconia* is giving expression to its faith — but that faith remains dead. Ultimately, such a community is incapable of finding God, since it has failed to see that God is to be found in human beings, especially in the poor (see Matt. 25). "We cannot share the eucharistic bread without sharing our daily bread too."[24]

The church is alive where the corporal works of mercy are performed: feeding the hungry, giving drink to the thirsty, clothing the naked, giving shelter to strangers, freeing captives, visiting the sick, and burying the dead. The church is likewise alive where the spiritual works of mercy are performed: correcting sinners, teaching the ignorant, giving good counsel to those in doubt, bearing patiently with those who are burdensome, gladly forgiving those who insult us, and praying for the living and the dead. If this diaconal dimension is taken seriously, there can be no such thing as "private" distress: the *communio* of the church means that everyone will show solidarity and be concerned about the distress of others. When one member rejoices, all the members rejoice; when one member suffers, all the members suffer with that member (1 Cor. 12:26). This is the logical consequence of our common existence in Christ and of our participation in the realization of his pastoral ministry. He came as the good shepherd who lays down his life for his sheep (John 10:11, 15). Accordingly, *diaconia* is not a subsidiary activity in a community or a hobby practiced by only a few. It is a central task of the Christian community, especially of church ministry, in imitation of Jesus and in obedience to the mission received from him.

We have seen that the church cannot exist without *diaconia*, since Christ himself is "one who serves [*diakonôn*]" (Luke 22:27). This is why he not only instituted the priestly ministry of service in the context of the Passover meal on the evening before his passion, but also founded the diaconal ministry. When he washed his disciples' feet, he gave us an example, that we might act in accordance with what he has done for us (John 13:15). One can see this logion as the institution of the diaconate, the ecclesial ministry that bestows a sacramental form on the close interconnection between *martyria*, *liturgia*, and *diaconia*. This does not dispense either the laity or bishops and priests from their own diaconal task. We must, however, inquire how the *diaconia* of the ecclesial ministry, which the deacon represents in a special manner, is related to the *diaconia* that the entire people of God, and all who wish to imitate Jesus, are called to exercise.

In *Lumen Gentium* 10 the council speaks of the common priesthood of all the baptized, and in *Sacrosanctum Concilium* 14 of the "active participation" (*actuosa participatio*) of the entire people of God; this concerns not only the liturgy, but every aspect of the church's life. This means that, although the essential difference between the clergy and the laity remains, our existence as the people of God, which is common to all the baptized, is antecedent to every differentiation of offices, charisms, and ministries.[25] "The church as *communio* must be understood as a differentiated totality, as a body or organism in which the various organs cooperate in varied manners for the good of the whole."[26]

The *communio*-ecclesiology thus bids farewell to a model of pastoral care in which the community is "looked after" and "its needs are provided for," since it means that all the members of the church share, each in their own way, in bearing responsibility in and for the church. But *corruptio optimi pessima*, "the worst corruption is the corruption of that which is best." There is scarcely any other aspect of the council's teaching that has been subject to such fundamental misunderstandings as this. The erroneous view that the *theological* reality of the "people of God" (*laos tou Theou*) is analogous to a national political entity (*dêmos*) has led to demands for the democratization of the church. If all that is meant is the request for a greater measure of participation, this is basically justified; but it is often motivated by the ideological desire to reduce the irreducible distinction between the various charisms, offices, and ministries. "What the council meant by 'people of God' was not the laity or grassroots as distinct from or even in opposition to the 'hierarchical church.' The people of God is the organic and structured totality of the church, the people assembled round its bishop and dependent on him, as Cyprian of Carthage put it."[27]

What is then the specific task of the ordained ministry within this totality? We find the clearest answer to this question in the Letter to the Ephesians, where we read that the exalted Lord in heaven has instituted the various offices: "that some should be apostles, some prophets, some evangelists, some pastors and teachers, to equip the saints [i.e., the believers] for the work of ministry, for building up the body of Christ" (4:11f.). Ecclesial office is a ministry to the other ministries, which it "equips" for service: it is not meant to suppress and crush the others, but rather to inspire, motivate, and train them to carry out their own tasks. This is how it contributes to the edification of the body of Christ, which consists of many members, many charisms and services. It is not meant to perform all the church's *diaconia*, nor could it ever do so. But it is meant to inspire, motivate, and train the others for diaconal service, and the best way to do so is to give the example of its own diaconal service, inviting others in its preaching to do the same and strengthening them on this path by means of the sacramental ministry.

Diaconia is an essential and foundational dimension of the church and a central aspect of the bishop's mission. The bishop commissions deacons to perform this task and gives them a share in his own office; in this way, they represent Jesus Christ, the good shepherd and deacon. Their diaconal ministry should inspire and enkindle others, encouraging them and strengthening them so that they too will imitate Jesus by serving their brothers and sisters, by sharing with them and helping them through the spiritual and corporal works of mercy, thus building up the community of Jesus Christ and realizing its unity in their lives. Hence, the ecclesiology of *communio* makes the ministry of the permanent deacon a necessity. He represents Jesus Christ, for he too is the good shepherd who goes in search of the strayed sheep, takes it on his shoulders and brings it back to the flock — and is willing to lay down his own life in the attempt.

Contemporary Relevance of *Communio-Diaconia*

The church and its communities live and work in the present time, and they must always pay heed to the signs of the times. Today, the church, like society as a whole, is experiencing a tremendous external and internal break in continuity. Deacons are called and challenged in a particular way to recognize the signs of the times and be attentive to the joy and hope, the sorrow and fear of their fellow human beings.[28] They must share these and attempt to bring healing; they must interpret them and put them into words, indicating the direction and orientation that faith provides and communicating to human beings in their daily lives the courage and strength, patience and hope, joy and peace that are the fruit of the Christian faith. I conclude this essay by inquiring into the relevance of the diaconal ministry in the present and the future: what does *communio-diaconia* mean today? We begin with a necessarily brief analysis of the present situation.

"Freedom" is perhaps the great word of the modern period, its most central and fundamental idea. For a long time, the church failed to acknowledge this word and the lofty value that it expresses; the church was slow to realize the Christian roots of this modern yearning and went so far as to condemn "freedom." A change in course came only with the Second Vatican Council, and one of the great achievements of the pontificate of John Paul II has been a consistent "politics of human rights," which has taken up and developed this conciliar heritage, deepening it and widening it and thus making a significant contribution to the birth of freedom in eastern Europe.

John Paul II has, however, never tired of insisting that the modern Western striving for freedom has a flip side. It is not by chance that this striving has generated the postmodern trend toward individualization, dethroning *fraternité* — the third great slogan of the French Revolution — and leading to a widespread refusal to practice solidarity. This is characterized by increasing loneliness, isolation, and coldness in society and the erosion of those shared values on which human fellowship is based; for when freedom is understood one-sidedly as emancipation, the result is a growing detachment from the fundamental values without which the modern history of freedom would never have been possible. This emancipatory "freedom from" — without "freedom for" — has given birth to a postmodern pluralism that enjoys the rank of a basic principle, and to an arbitrariness that is no longer capable of enthusiasm or of making a decision in favor of something positive, since it is indifferent and skeptical vis-à-vis all allegedly ultimate values. This causes a deficit in meaningfulness, an intellectual vacuum, and an inner emptiness that ends in meaninglessness and nihilism.

This societal situation is marked by phenomena such as the increase of tension, loneliness, and boredom in marriage and family life; there is a constant increase in the divorce statistics and in the number of single parents. In the larger societal sphere we find material poverty and unemployment, the distress of refugees and displaced persons, the homeless, addicts, lonely and despairing persons, those incapable of forming stable relationships, women and children exposed to violence, and those who live on the margins of society and risk turning to crime. It seems as if a collective inability to form relationships, indeed an inability to live, threatens our society; its symptoms are loneliness, isolation, destructiveness, and a refusal to get involved, aphasia and fear of contact with others. Life has grown darker for many people, while others are victims of a resigned depression in the face of threats to their physical existence or their psychological stability.

Other signs of the times are a drop-out mentality on the one hand and a willingness to drift with the flow on the other: the reality of people's lives is contradictory. Other persons again are manipulated by advertising and the media, so that they bow down before false images of life. This leads them to make excessive demands on themselves and on others; the outcome is only frustration and disappointment. We also see many who live in unbridled prosperity and luxury, pursuing pleasure with no thought of others and aggressively imposing their own will at all costs. These too are signs of the times.[29]

The social background that I have sketched here helps us grasp why young people experience a new yearning for *communio*, which they understand initially as fellowship. They want to overcome isolation and loneliness and to form relationships, and they long for peace and reconciliation. However, *communio* also means participation: they want to belong. An outward expression of this longing is the conformity to fashion, but this is not merely an external matter: those who wear the same clothes, use the same language, and adopt the same kind of behavior are signaling that they want to belong and that they share the same attitudes. Unlike the customs and traditions of earlier times, however, fashion is an unreliable basis — by definition, what is fashionable today is *passé* tomorrow. Accordingly, there exists a deeper search for meaning, which also takes the form of religious movements. These are often vague and ill-defined; they remain on the general level and frequently fail to connect with the great stream of ecclesial tradition. Nevertheless, they exist, and it is possible for the church to enter a dialogue with them. Indeed, this is often what such movements themselves desire.

This situation makes an urgent appeal to the *communio-diaconia*. It is here that its task lies, for it is the deacon's special call to be on the front line, an attentive listener and a pioneer who leads the church's response to these challenges. As a married man and father, the deacon can often find it easier to make contact with people than a celibate priest. This is why deacons should not seek to take over as large a slice as possible of the specifically priestly ministry of leadership: their task is different, and it is important and urgent enough! For before a community can be guided and before the Eucharist can be celebrated in it and with it, it must first be gathered together and built up. The deacon's place is in these marginal areas of church and society, where breakthroughs can occur. He is not to think only of those who "still" belong to the church and to accompany them, but also to invite those who perhaps may belong to the church tomorrow. His *communio-diaconia* means that he builds up the church in view of the future. This is an absolutely essential contribution to the "new evangelization" about which we hear so much today.

Apart from the social distress, which is also reflected in the life of our parishes, there exists a specific ecclesial distress connected with the form of the church and its communities and many forms of pastoral care. This too poses a challenge to the deacon. The church's history is a heavy burden, and many people are wary when they encounter a church that finds it difficult to accept the new feeling of freedom and the widespread new religiosity. Many Catholics, including an increasing number of women, have given up practicing their faith and participating in parish life.

The diaconal dimension is often virtually absent from church life, and the link between *diaconia* and preaching and the liturgy often leaves much to be desired. Parishes seldom complain about the lack of diaconal activities, however — although they protest vigorously when a Mass must be dropped from the parish program or catechetical instruction is no longer given. We frequently hear about the "shortage of priests," but I have yet to hear anyone lament the "shortage of deacons." In the sphere of *diaconia*, nearly everything is delegated from the parish sphere to church institutions of various kinds, and *diaconia* was seldom in view when the permanent diaconate was introduced. "At any rate, one must be skeptical about the way in which the diaconate was reintroduced here in Germany. The enormous investment of theological, spiritual, and financial resources has not given any serious impetus to *diaconia* in the parishes or in the organized charitable work of the church. It has not proved possible to link *caritas* and pastoral care in this new ministry."[30]

This analysis might seem depressing, but we should not forget that difficult situations also entail opportunities and positive challenges. Here the question is how we can renew the form of the church and of its communities, so that the result is a church of *communio*, not obsessed with itself and its own problems, but concerned above all with the kingdom of God. For such a church, "the path to be taken is the human person" (to quote John Paul II). It has been shown that the public image of the church depends primarily on *diaconia*, and the diaconal work of the church enjoys the highest measure of respect in society. Since actions are more convincing than anything else, diaconal pastoral care is missionary pastoral care.

One reason why the traditional form of ecclesiastical offices and ministries no longer meets contemporary needs is that it can no longer ensure that the *diaconia* of Christ continues to be performed adequately. As we have seen, this is why the council made possible the renewal of the diaconate: the urgent needs of human persons and of the Christian communities virtually forced the renewal of this ministry, which entailed at the same time a renewed awareness that *diaconia* is a characteristic of the church as a whole and of all its ministries.

Some Concrete Observations on the Form of the Diaconate Today

In the light of these fundamental theological reflections and of what I have written about today's situation, I should like to make some concrete observations on the form of the diaconate, beginning with the basic spiritual attitude of the deacon. In St. John's Gospel, Jesus says: "It is the Spirit that gives life; the flesh is of no avail" (6:63). Institutional and structural reforms too can be "useless flesh" (to use this biblical image), if they are not borne up by the life-giving Spirit. This is why the renewal of the diaconate is first of all a spiritual task. The basic spiritual attitude of the deacon must make it clear that the Christian path is not an ascent or a triumphal march in glory, but a path that looks downward, following Jesus Christ, who descended from heaven. This "downwardly mobile career" is described in the christological hymn in the Letter to the Philippians (2:6–11), which prescribes the basic Christian virtue, as the spiritual tradition teaches, namely, the attitude of humility, which is a willingness to serve. This must *a fortiori* be the basic attitude of the deacon.

This includes a perceptive eye for those suffering distress, illness, or fear. The task is to bring a healing that sets free and empowers them to trust and so to serve and love others in their turn, as we see very clearly in Jesus' encounter with Peter's mother-in-law (Matt. 8:14f.). She lies sick in bed, unable to lead her own life, still less to care for anyone else. Jesus comes and sees this woman with his perceptive eye — seeing and perceiving are essential elements of what he does. He bends down to the sick woman without speaking, takes hold of her hand, and raises her up. She rises and stands on her own feet. Then she exercises *diaconia* (see the Greek text) by turning to others and "serving" them.

Now that she stands on her own feet, she can help others to stand on theirs.

Hence, we can say that "the goal of diaconal activity is...not simply help, but the empowering of life, so that those who lie prostrate may get to their feet. Naturally, we must look beyond individuals to perceive the social situations in which they live."[31] In some situations, the deacon can and must become the public advocate of the weak and powerless and of all those who have no other voice or lobby.

The concrete tasks must be tackled on the basis of these fundamental spiritual attitudes. The deacon is the contact partner for the various problems described above, and all those in need must be able to look confidently to him for help. Since his ministry includes liturgy, preaching, and *diaconia*, he can make others aware of the connection between faith and life. In his ministry at the altar, he lays the needs of human beings on the eucharistic table, and naturally he also speaks of these needs when he preaches. He must make the parish aware of urgent situations of need, motivating them to share with one another and to give practical help.

One essential task consists in finding, training, and guiding volunteer church workers. As time goes on, he must leave more and more tasks and services to these volunteers, concentrating more on accompanying them professionally, personally, and spiritually, since those who work in institutions such as kindergartens, health and counseling centers, or old people's homes themselves need pastoral care and guidance. Ideally, the deacon should initiate and support self-help groups, e.g., for single parents or drug addicts. It is clear that the contemporary problems described above are not restricted to any one community alone — the drug problem does not stop at the parish boundaries. "Open" work among young people normally cuts across such boundaries.

This perspective has led to the suggestion that although the deacon should be assigned to one specific parish and be integrated into its life, his ministry should have a wider scope, e.g., for a city, a deanery, or a region. With his base in one parish, he could build up the diaconal tasks in several communities and link these in a network. The emphasis here must lie on finding, training, accompanying, and supporting volunteer church workers in the individual parishes and setting up a network within one city or region. Such a project has already been successfully initiated in the diocese of Rottenburg-Stuttgart, and it entails great opportunities for the permanent diaconate.

Through his participation in ecclesial ministry, the deacon also shares in the leadership of the community, where his primary concern is to integrate *diaconia* and see that it is given its appropriate place in pastoral work.

As the official representative of the community, he is the obvious contact person for regional Catholic charity organizations and health centers. He should be represented in ecumenical diaconal associations. He should also ensure that the communities are in contact with those responsible for social matters in local government and in nongovernmental aid organizations. "The situation in our society has become...so complicated, and there are so many different kinds of problems, that the only way to cope with them is through the resolute and confident collaboration of professional Catholic charity workers, local grassroots initiatives, Caritas committees in the individual parishes, and parish *diaconia*."[32]

Many of these tasks can be done only by full-time professionals, others by a nonstipendiary deacon,[33] whose main opportunities lie in his professional activity where — like the French worker-priests — he should represent the church locally in his work and be present in spheres of life to which no one else from the church has access. He should then bring these experiences back into the community, where he is the advocate of *diaconia*. In this way, he would exercise his own autonomous ministry in an appropriate manner; he would not simply be an emergency replacement where priests are few in number.

Naturally, the parish is not the only ideal place for the deacon to work. Ministry to specific groups —

hospitals, old age homes, industrial chaplaincies, prisons, refugee hostels, etc. — can also be very suitable, as well as collaboration in the government of a diocese in those areas primarily concerned with diaconal leadership tasks. The deacons of a diocese also form an advisory body that can be very helpful to the bishop; as a fellowship, they can be the bishop's eyes and ears with respect to human needs, and they can help him to be the "father of the poor." Obviously, deacons must have the appropriate training that qualifies them for such work.

I close with a thought that may at first sight seem utopian. The church cannot exist without *diaconia*, and the church indeed has a particular office for *diaconia*. Therefore, would it not make sense for each parish to have a deacon? This would not involve any financial problem, since one could install nonstipendiary deacons. I believe that every parish contains undiscovered potential in this area: ideally, the priest and the community would suggest to the bishop, or to those with responsibility for the diaconate in his diocese, that such and such a person would be a good candidate for the ministry of nonstipendiary deacon.

In the diocese of Besançon they have gone even further than this. Those responsible for the diaconate attend meetings in the deaneries, which are invited to reflect on the urgent social problems that exist in their region and to look for suitable men who could work in these areas as nonstipendiary deacons. These men are then asked if they are willing to be ordained and are given a year to think about the question. If their answer is positive, their training begins. I find this an inspiring model.

In conclusion: spiritually motivated, well-trained deacons employed in meaningful tasks are a necessity for the church today. They are neither substitutes for a parish priest nor social workers. They represent the deacon Jesus Christ in a sacramental manner, bringing into our world the love of God, which the Holy Spirit has poured out into our hearts (Rom. 5:5). They are pioneers of a new "civilization of love." They are a blessing for the church and for the people entrusted to us. This is why we must press on with renewal of *diaconia* and of the diaconate, translating ever more fully into the reality of ecclesial life the impetus given by the Holy Spirit through the Second Vatican Council.

- 2 -

Priestly Office

Recent Discussions of the Topic

In the last few decades, the priestly ministry in virtually all the Western European churches has been in a crisis. In most dioceses, the considerable decline in the numbers of seminarians and newly ordained priests raises concern, and the situation will worsen in the coming years, once those ordained in great numbers retire from active ministry. Another cause for concern is that priests are abandoning their ministry. Many priests feel that their burden is too heavy to bear and that their work shows little sign of success. This mood leads to resignation and frustration, which in their turn can lead to aggression. While most priests carry out their ministry well and gladly, one cannot fail to note that these feelings — especially in very young priests — rob the Christian message (which is meant to be liberating "good news") of its attractiveness and render sterile much that an excessive activism builds up.

The contemporary crisis has many sources, and one must beware of glib simplifications that try to reduce it to a single cause. There can be no doubt that the difficulties and failures experienced by priests, and the opposition and malice of a secularized milieu largely indifferent to religion, play a role here. But we should search for causes not only outside the church; we should begin by examining life in the church itself, whose general climate is experienced by many, and perhaps the majority of priests, as depressing. The German bishops in their 1992 Letter on priestly ministry attempted to provide an open and honest analysis of this situation; priests felt they were understood, and they were grateful for the bishops' expression of solidarity. At any rate, this document was more effective than yet another purely theoretical, dogmatic-theological clarification of the "image" of the priest.

However, we cannot overlook that one cause of the present difficulties results from theological confusions and distortions. More precisely, it is rooted in a superficial and one-sided reception of the ecclesiology of the Second Vatican Council, which emphasized the "people of God" and *communio*, and the associated doctrine of the common priesthood of all the baptized. This ecclesiology generated the question, especially in the first phase of discussion after the council, of how the *proprium* and *specificum* of the official priestly ministry are to be defined, given that all the baptized are called to share in the priestly people of God. A second cause of the lack of theological clarity is ideological and arose in the wake of the cultural revolution of the 1960s and early 1970s. This consists of a transposition of democratic ideas to the church without any attempt at differentiation and is often linked to a broad ideological critique and distrust of institutions; naturally, this attitude is found not only in the church, but also in society as a whole.

This suffices to show that the discussion about ecclesial ministry is only the tip of an iceberg. Ultimately, the question is about the very essence of the church, or the obscuring and undermining of the image of the church that the last council derived from Scripture and tradition.

This perspective is important, since it can preserve us from falling victim to a logical fallacy. We are often told that all these questions can be resolved more or less pragmatically, e.g., by reorganizing pastoral care through uniting parishes or grouping them together, or by delegating to laypersons tasks traditionally carried out by priests (including the task of community leadership). No doubt, much can and must be resolved pragmatically; but one should also bear in mind that purely pragmatic solutions are often like comets, trailing theological implications and consequences in their wake. For those of us who have studied theology, many clear and subtle distinctions have a certain degree of plausibility; but the faithful will either fail to understand them, despite all their efforts, or else reject them as nothing more than theological hair-splitting or verbal smokescreens. If we wish to avoid misunderstandings, we must think through the problems on the level of basic principles.

This also applies to the widespread view that one could resolve the question by changing the so-called conditions of admittance to the priestly ministry. Such a position fails to recognize that our real problem is not a shortage of priests, but a shortage of faithful and of communities — and that this in turn is one of the causes of the shortage of priests.

Like the other pragmatic solutions I have mentioned, this proposal too seems at first sight very progressive. However, its underlying goal is merely the preservation of the status quo: it is not open to a deeper renewal of our understanding of the church and to a transformation of our concrete pastoral practice. I am firmly convinced that the contemporary crisis must not be seen only in the light of its negative aspects: we could also consider it a *kairos* for developing, if not a new church, then at any rate a new epochal form of our church as it enters the third millennium of its history. We ought to attempt to go beyond apologetics and find a constructive and creative path, step by step, to a solution to our problems.

The Representative Character of the Apostolic Office

The theme of *repraesentatio Christi capitis* brings us to the theological basis and heart of the Catholic understanding of church ministry, and especially of the priestly office, which was authoritatively summarized by the magisterium in the decree *Presbyterorum Ordinis* of the Second Vatican Council "On the Ministry and Life of Priests."

Here I cannot take up all the many complicated exegetical and historical questions concerning the genesis of the church's ministries; much has been written on this subject, and many helpful contributions have been published in the last twenty years. It is beyond dispute that developments took place within the New Testament itself and that these reached a kind of conclusion in the immediately postapostolic or even postbiblical period (e.g., in Ignatius of Antioch); many further developments took place subsequently, and it is clear that developments are taking place today too, on the basis of previous tradition.

It is not difficult to understand that the early writings and strata of the New Testament display a certain lack of clarity on this point: it lies in the nature of things that one can speak of institutionalized offices, and more so of a reflection on such ministries, only in the second generation. Nevertheless, we do not risk oversimplification if we take our starting point in the fact — perfectly well attested in historical terms — that official ministries did not arrive on the scene at some later stage as a deviant form of "early Catholic" development in contrast to an original community structure that was either purely charismatic or (as some think, in defiance of historical evidence) purely democratic. There was never any initial period without ministries: these are as old as the church itself, and they have been conferred by the laying on of hands since the apostolic age.

The words of the apostle Paul in 2 Corinthians 5:14–20 are a particularly eloquent demonstration of the essential link that the New Testament witness posits between the *res* of the Gospel and the official service of the Gospel; neither of these is posterior to the other. Paul speaks in this chapter first of the heart of the Gospel, namely, Jesus' surrender of himself to death and his resurrection that has made all things new. Then he adds in v. 18: "God through Christ reconciled us to himself and gave us [i.e., the apostles] the ministry of reconciliation." As Gisbert Greshake has written, God posited the ministry of reconciliation along with the decisive salvific deed of reconciliation. God's salvific deed and the service of this deed must be seen as belonging together in one single event.

The Bible sees the deepest ground for this unity in the indissoluble link between the witness that is borne and the witness who bears it. This link reaches its highest concentration in the Christ event, since it is impossible to detach the *res* of Jesus Christ, his message that God's kingdom has drawn near, from his person. He is in person that which he proclaims. To use Origen's word, he is the *autobasileia*, the God who has drawn near to us, God's self-communication in person; to use the language of the dogmatic tradition, he is in person the unity between God and human being. Nor is his resurrection from the dead a "fact" that one could investigate and confirm independently of the testimony of the first witnesses. As Heinrich Schlier has shown, the empty tomb is only a sign, an indication, a trace of the raising of Jesus from the dead. The Easter faith cannot be detached from the Easter testimony of the apostolic witnesses who were called and sent out to attest this message (though this does not mean that Rudolf Bultmann was correct to dissolve the Easter faith into this testimony, and to affirm that Jesus arose "only" into the kerygma). The constitutive element in Paul's concept of "apostle" is the fact that the risen Lord had appeared to certain persons who had been determined beforehand by God, and had sent them out to preach.[1] Since the Easter faith is tied to the Easter testimony, one cannot proclaim faith in Jesus Christ to one's own self; one cannot work this out for oneself by studying or amassing knowledge. Faith in Christ is no abstract idea, nor a hypostasis that could be detached from the concrete event of proclamation and the community of faith. Faith in Jesus Christ is proclaimed and attested to us with authority by one who is given the charge and mission to do so. Faith in Jesus is tied to the apostolic ministry.

Since this unity between the testimony to faith and the human witness to faith is an essential structure of Christian believing, it cannot cease to exist when the last of the apostles dies: their mission is meant to last "until the end of the age" (Matt. 28:20). Accordingly, it is necessary that others enter this mission and exercise it after the apostles' deaths. While it is not possible for new apostles to take the place of the first apostles, there must always be others who carry out fundamental apostolic functions and make the apostolic mission a present reality down through the ages.

The christological unity between the testimony and the human witness allows us to go on to make a fundamental affirmation about the essence of the apostolic office: if Jesus Christ is his *res* in person, then the testimony to him and to his *res* cannot be detached from the apostolic office; more important still, this office cannot be detached in any way from Jesus Christ himself. This is why the expression "Gospel of Jesus Christ" in the New Testament means not only "the Gospel that speaks of Jesus Christ" (an objective genitive) but also, indeed primarily, "the Gospel that is Jesus Christ," the Gospel in which Jesus Christ in person bears witness to himself and in which he himself is salvifically present (a subjective genitive). One may borrow Augustine's well-known language and say: *Christus est qui praedicat, qui baptizat, qui consecrat.*[2] Just as Jesus Christ is the primary celebrant of the sacraments, so he is also the primary and the real teacher and shepherd in the church. This is why the Tübingen school spoke of Jesus Christ's "handing on of himself" (*Selbstüberlieferung*) in the Holy Spirit. In the light of this insight, we may say that Jesus Christ, the risen and exalted Lord, gives utterance to his own self when his apostles speak: through their ministry, he hands on his own self.

This is precisely what the apostle Paul says in 2 Corinthians 5:20: "So we are ambassadors for Christ, God making his appeal through us. We beseech you on behalf of Christ, be reconciled to God!" When testimony is borne to the Gospel, the true actor is Jesus Christ — but he acts through the mediation of his witnesses, who do not take the place of an "absent" Lord, but allow him to speak as one who is genuinely present. The apostolic witnesses are not an intermediary: what they mediate is an immediacy to Jesus Christ. To put this somewhat differently, the apostolic office has a real-symbolic function, representing the one to whom the apostles bear witness. Jesus Christ is salvifically present in and through the apostolic ministries.

This idea of representation is found in another form in the New Testament, namely, in the *shaliach* (missionary) formulae that are inseparably linked to the concept of apostle. In Jewish law, the one sent has the same status as the one who sends him. This is why Jesus can say: "He who hears you hears me, and he who rejects you rejects me, and he who rejects me rejects him who sent me" (Luke 10:16).

The Pauline epistles employ yet another concept to articulate this idea: here we frequently read of the eternal salvific counsel (*mustêrion*) that was hidden in God and then realized in Jesus Christ and made manifest in the apostle's preaching.[3] This makes the apostolic ministry a constitutive element of God's eternal mystery of salvation in Jesus Christ, in and through whom this mystery is revealed in history. The apostle Paul is permeated by this idea of representation to such an extent that he can call his own apostolic journeys Christ's triumphal march through the world (2 Cor. 2:14). Indeed, it is not only his preaching but his entire apostolic existence that is determined *in toto* by this idea: "always carrying in the body the death of Jesus, so that the life of Jesus also may be manifested in our bodies" (2 Cor. 4:10). The apostle understands himself, in his apostolic sufferings, as the very epiphany of his Lord and of the new life of Jesus that overcomes death. Thus the essential structure inherent in the apostolic ministry has the sacramental dimension of a sign.

The Apostolic Office: Representation of Jesus Christ as Head of the Church

One may in a certain sense say that every Christian is called to the *repraesentatio Christi*. All baptized persons have clothed themselves in Christ; they live in Christ and Christ lives in them, and each Christian can and should bear witness to Christ in word and deed and make him present to other Christians. According to the Second Vatican Council, all the baptized share in the threefold office of Jesus Christ and form a prophetic, priestly, and kingly people (1 Pet. 2:5–10). This is what is meant when we speak of the common priesthood of all the baptized. Finally, the church as a whole is the body of Christ, and hence the representation of Christ in the world; as a whole, the church is a sacrament, i.e., God's sign and instrument in and for the world.

As we have seen, one consequence of this emphasis on the common responsibility of all Christians has been an uncertainty that leads to the question: What remains of the ministry? What is its specific character? Is it anything more than a representation of the community or the church, and of the will of the majority that is manifested in the church?

The theology of the apostle Paul offers a very clear answer to this question: the fact that responsibility is shared does not mean that everyone in the church can do everything, or that all together can do everything.[4] A passage in the Letter to the Ephesians illustrates the special task of the ministry within the body of Christ as a whole. Here, Paul explains how the risen Lord establishes the various forms of service from heaven, i.e., "from above." Paul mentions "apostles, prophets, evangelists, pastors, and teachers," and we should note how Ephesians defines the special task of these ministries: they are "to equip the saints [i.e., the Christians] for the work of ministry, for building up the body of Christ" (4:12). Accordingly, the special task of ministerial service is to equip the other forms of service to serve; it serves the other services and helps thereby to build up the whole body of Christ. It is a spiritual, pastoral service of the individual members of the church and of the church as a whole. This means that the essential structure inherent in the apostolic ministry includes a sacramental dimension with the character of a sign.

Behind this specific task of the official ministry lies the conviction that individual Christians do not simply "possess" their own charism; nor does the church, as Christ's body, owe its life to itself or to its own power. The Christian existence and the life of the church are possible only thanks to Jesus Christ, the Head of the church. He did not found and equip the church once and for all, so that it could now get on with things on its own; in all that they do, both the church and every individual Christian owe their life completely to the Lord who is present in his body. Their life comes not "from below," but "from above," since "Christ is the Head, from whom the whole body, joined and knit together by every joint with which it is supplied, when each part is working properly, makes bodily growth and upbuilds itself in love" (Eph. 4:16).

This leads us to the all-important thesis that the service of the official ministry is addressed both to individuals and to the church as a whole. As such, it is a *repraesentatio* of the ministry that Jesus Christ, its Head, performs for the church, keeping it alive, nourishing it, purifying, sanctifying, leading, guiding, governing, unifying it, and keeping it together. The official ministry is not only *repraesentatio Christi* in some general sense; it is *repraesentatio Christi capitis Ecclesiae*.

According to the teaching of the last council, the bishops, as successors of the apostles, possess in plenitude this apostolic ministry in the full sense of the term;[5] priests share in this mission of the bishops and are called their collaborators, helpers, and instruments, as well as their sons, brothers, and friends.[6] They are to represent the bishop in the local community[7] and make him present there.[8] In today's situation, it is important to recall this connection between the priestly and the episcopal ministry, since it is often objected that priests who come to celebrate the Eucharist in a parish where there is no pastor are merely "itinerant consecrators" who do not in fact exercise the ministry of unity and community edification in this parish. If we take seriously the principle that it is the bishop who is the true head of each community, it follows that any priest can represent the bishop locally, in virtue of his priestly ordination; where the bishop gives him this commission, any priest can share in the leadership of any particular parish community.

In his dissertation, Paul Cordes has shown that precisely this idea of the *repraesentatio Christi capitis* is the fundamental idea at the heart of the conciliar decree *Presbyterorum Ordinis*. We read in §6: "Priests exercise the function of Christ as Pastor and Head in proportion to their authority," and in §12: "By the sacrament of Order priests are configured to Christ the priest as servants of the Head, so that as co-workers with the episcopal order they may build up the Body of Christ." Through this *repraesentatio Christi capitis*, the ecclesial ministry attests that the church draws its life not from its own self, but from Jesus Christ. The ministry reminds us that salvation is not derived from anything in the world, but is the grace God offers when he speaks to his people. The ministry bears witness to Jesus Christ who always goes ahead, and to the prevenient salvation that he accomplishes. In other words, the ministry stands for the real substance of the Christian message. It is not itself this substance; in essence, it is an indicator, a sign, and an instrument that points away from and above itself. As such, however, it is a constitutive element of the very event of salvation, which it makes present in the temporal dimension.

The Apostolic Ministry as Representation of the Church

What we have written about the position of the ministry vis-à-vis the church or the community does not completely describe this relationship. Our starting point hitherto has been the mission that Jesus receives from the Father and that includes both the apostles and the apostolic office, but the event of salvation is characterized not only by this descending (or "katabatic") line; there is also the ascending (or "anabatic") line, the movement that leads through Jesus Christ in the Holy Spirit to the Father. When Jesus Christ gives life to the church, sanctifies it, and leads it through the Holy Spirit, he does not crush or manipulate it; rather, he liberates it and empowers it to make the response of thanksgiving (*eucharistia*) to the Father through himself in the Holy Spirit. This ascending line is also important for our understanding of the church's ministry: here we might compare it to the director of a choir or to the spokesperson of the entire community of the faithful who are given life by the Holy Spirit.

This aspect is expressed with particular clarity in the account of the so-called apostolic council in Jerusalem (Acts 15), where Luke describes a living cooperation between the apostles and the community. Paul too, though possessing an unparalleled conviction that he had been directly sent by the risen Lord, attaches great importance to confirmation by the faith of his communities: he wishes not only to strengthen them, but also to be strengthened and supported by their faith (Rom. 1:12). This mutual relationship finds its clearest expression precisely in the passage in which Paul most clearly says that he works "in the place of Christ." Here he is not content merely to issue commands in the name of Christ: he begs the Corinthian community, "Let yourselves be reconciled to God!" (2 Cor. 5:20).

This dual character can be seen with particular clarity in the Eucharist, where the priest acts in a special way *in persona Christi* — since otherwise, he could not say: "This is my body... this is my blood" — but also speaks in the name of the church, offering the sacrifice of praise as the church's spokesman and leader. Otherwise, as Peter Lombard long ago observed, he would have to say *offero* in the singular rather than *offerimus* in the plural.[9] This is why the Roman canon says, "Father, we celebrate the memory of Christ, your Son. We, your people and your ministers, recall his passion...." The Second Vatican Council formulated this double function unambiguously in its constitution on the church: "In the person of Christ, the ministerial priest effects the eucharistic sacrifice and offers it to God in the name of all the people."[10]

The tradition is profoundly marked by the insight that the ministry represents the church and acts on its behalf. We cannot present here all the testimonies that Yves Congar assembled in his book on the laity; we must be content with quoting the affirmation of Bishop Cyprian, "The bishop is in the church and the church is in the bishop."[11] Augustine summarized in other terms the tension entailed by the double position of the ecclesial office-bearer: "For you I am a bishop, with you I am a Christian."[12] And Thomas Aquinas, for all his emphasis on the basic proposition that the priest acts *in persona Christi*, frequently says that the ministry represents the church.[13]

These were not purely theoretical affirmations; they acquired a practical significance in the church's tradition, as we see in the participation of the people in the election of their bishop and in the principle that no one should be ordained bishop against the will of the people (see Celestine I and Leo the Great). Cyprian makes the general declaration that he wishes to do nothing without the counsel of the clergy and the assent of the laity.[14] This means that ministers cannot complacently ignore the people and enforce their own will; even Pius XII emphasized the right of the laity to express their opinion publicly in the church. Where this connection between ministers and laypersons is no longer maintained, office-bearers become a caricature of themselves, as "shepherds who merely pasture their own selves" (Ezek. 34:2). The responsibility of the ministers is neither exclusive nor universal; it is inherently related to the other charisms, which it must complete and strengthen, and ministers must be open to inspiration — and sometimes to criticism — from others in the church. Hence, the last council was right to put an end to the obsessive concentration on the clergy; its texts urge the pastors to listen to the laity, in the hope that a new intimacy on both sides will bear much fruit for the church.[15] This lays the foundations of the various bodies in which all Christians can exercise their common responsibility; the most important institutional expression here is the pastoral council. This is the theological justification for the thesis (also found in texts of the magisterium) that the parish and its pastor are the joint subject of pastoral care.

This is not paying tribute to the democratic *Zeitgeist*, but the concrete articulation of the ecclesiology of Vatican II with its emphasis on the "people of God" and *communio*. Naturally, the church is not a democracy — but nor is it characterized exclusively by its hierarchical structure! In the past, the church adopted a number of feudal and monarchical elements in order to provide a concrete articulation for its own constitution. In the same way, it can and must take up some democratic structural elements and procedures today, in a manner both critical and creative, in order to express in the forms appropriate to human law its own constitution, which is prescribed antecedently to the church's action, since it belongs to the sphere of divine law and hence is inviolable. I do not have the impression that the implications of Vatican II have been fully realized as yet; these questions have still to be discussed in depth.

The Task of Leading the Community

The concept of "community leadership" is often employed today to express the reality that we have described in biblical terms and set out in simple theological language. This phrase admittedly sounds rather functionalistic, and it remains somewhat placid if it is not understood in its full theological sense. If we take seriously all that has been written above, the leadership of a community means more, theologically speaking, than just organization and administration, the "management" of a parish. Clearly administration and management are necessary in the church, which is not of this world, but nevertheless lives in this world; to call this into question would be a sign of a spiritualistic ecclesiology. In the theological sense, however, community leadership goes further and deeper, since it means building up a community in the commission received from Jesus Christ and in his power, with Jesus himself as the criterion of our work. The community is built up when it is nourished from the table of the Word and the table of the Eucharist, when it is purified and sanctified, when it is empowered and motivated to perform its own service in the world, and when the charisms that are at work in the community are integrated with one another and kept united to the church as a whole.

Many titles are used in Scripture to describe the way in which Jesus Christ builds up the community: he is called prophet and teacher, priest, lord, shepherd, and king. The plurality of titles expresses the variety of ways in which Jesus Christ exercises the headship of his church, and these have been summarized, first in Protestant theology, then by M. J. Scheeben in the nineteenth century, and later at Vatican II, in the ministerial triad of "prophet, priest, and shepherd." The office-bearer shares in a particular way in this threefold ministry of Christ, and this means that community leadership takes the threefold form of preaching, the celebration of the sacraments (especially the Eucharist), and the exercise of the pastoral office.

This articulation of the one ministry of Jesus Christ, of the church, and of the ecclesial office allowed the last council to supersede the medieval restriction of ministry to a cultic priesthood and an episcopal office that was understood in purely jurisdictional terms. The council wished to reestablish a closer link between the authority derived from ordination (*ordo*) and the authority to exercise governance (*iurisdictio*), displaying their inherent unity and associating them closely with the commission to proclaim the Gospel.

This concern of the Second Vatican Council is directly relevant to our own discussion, since it means that leadership of the community cannot be detached from the ministry of presiding at the Eucharist, the sacrament of unity. Accordingly, the Mass is not only the center and summit of the community's life, but also the central act of community leadership. Nor can one detach the ministry of the community leader from the ministries of the preacher and the good shepherd who keeps the flock together and makes it a priority to search for the lost. Neither the purely "cultic" priest who rushes in his automobile from one Mass to the next nor the clerical supermanager is in accordance with the model proposed by the council in the light of Scripture and tradition: community leadership in the full theological sense demands that the proclamation of the Word, the celebration of the sacraments, and pastoral service form a unity. The priest attests his identification with Jesus Christ, not only through his ministerial activity, but through his whole existence. Accordingly, his threefold service makes him in his innermost being the source of the community's identity:[16] he helps it to identify with Jesus Christ and to grow "to the measure of the stature of the fullness of Christ" (Eph. 4:13). He cannot do this if he is *only* the one who is in charge of the community; he must also lead it in its prayer, since his service of leadership is a spiritual service.

As a spiritual service, community leadership cannot be exercised in an autocratic manner; it must collaborate with the other ministries and with the entire community, and it is in this context that the term "cooperative pastoral care" has been coined. This corresponds to the relationship between Jesus and his disciples. He behaves not as their lord, but "as one who serves" (Luke 22:25–27), and calls them "no longer servants, but friends" (John 15:15). Leadership of a community in the name of Jesus makes demands on the office-bearer himself, before it makes any demands on others. The exercise of authority in the name of Jesus means exercising authority as Jesus did: "We do not lord it over your faith; we work with you for your joy" (2 Cor. 1:24).

In their Letter about the priestly ministry, the German bishops made this point by affirming that it is not a "production," but rather a "representation." A productive service makes or changes something, and we can point to what we have done; in the modern period, human activity is almost exclusively a question of productive praxis. Pastoral work, however, cannot do this: there is nothing here for us to "make." As priests, all we can do is offer ourselves for the purpose of representation. We are signs of something that we ourselves cannot effect, and it is essential that we are transparent to that which (or better, to the one whom) we represent. As priests, we must not take center-stage: we must be hearers and doers of the Word. Priestly existence is existence as a witness and a sign, not only with our lips, but with the whole of our existence. Since we ourselves are less important than the *res* to which we must bear testimony, and our fundamental attitude must be the refusal to "possess" and to "produce," the evangelical counsels — not only celibacy, but also poverty and obedience — are the appropriate form of life for the one who exercises community leadership in this theological sense.

Collaboration by Laypersons in Tasks of Community Leadership

This brings us to an urgent practical problem: at present (and for the foreseeable future), there are too few celibate priests available to exercise the ministry of community leadership that is so vital for the church. What are we to do? Asking one priest to care for several parishes is certainly not the solution, for this makes excessive physical, human, and spiritual demands on most priests. In order to cope with this dramatic problem, many have suggested entrusting community leadership to laypersons, whether salaried[17] or not (e.g., the chairperson of the parish council, or a team of laity).

In view of what I have written above, we must affirm that community leadership in the theological sense is possible only for one who is ordained, since it cannot be divorced from the celebration of the Eucharist. Such a dichotomy would reduce community leadership to a purely functional service, thus reintroducing the fatal separation between *ordo* and *iurisdictio* and reversing one of the most important developments at Vatican II.

I believe that the council indicates another path out of our difficulties when it takes up the references in the New Testament to those men and women who collaborated with the apostle Paul.[18] It is clear that they played an important role in the earliest communities, and Paul employs exactly the same concepts to speak of their work and of the activity of office-bearers, namely, "serving" and "toiling." Indeed, he states that the two men Andronicus and Junias (or, following a reading often preferred today, the man Andronicus and the woman Junia) are respected apostles in the communities (Rom. 16:7). This allows the council to elaborate the basic outlines of a theology of pastoral collaborators, which unfortunately has been little heeded and further developed in the past decades. The primary affirmation here is that laypersons' sharing in the salvific mission of the church, which is rooted in their baptism, can include the call to direct collaboration in the apostolate of the hierarchy. Thanks to their own *missio*, the laity can assume the exercise of particular tasks (*munia*) that are more closely linked with the ministries (*officia*) of the pastors, in teaching, in liturgical actions, and in pastoral work (*cura animarum*). In this context, the council speaks of a *cooperatio* in the exercise of specific ministries that, however, does not entail a *participatio* in the hierarchical ministry itself.[19]

These indications require more precise articulation, but even so, it is clear that the council did not accept the thesis that echoes Karl Rahner by declaring that everyone who exercises some particular function in the church has an immediate share in the ecclesial ministry itself; Edward Schillebeeckx has taken this thesis further and maintained that in situations of necessity, laypersons can also celebrate an "emergency Eucharist." Nor does the council go in the direction of establishing new ministries, in the sense that the introduction of salaried "pastoral assistants" would have created a new grade of the sacrament of orders. For the council, these pastoral collaborators remain laypersons — but laypersons with a special official *missio* authorizing them to collaborate in the exercise of specific tasks that belong to the ordained ministry.

Postconciliar canon law took up these conciliar declarations and made it possible for laypersons to receive a specific commission to collaborate in particular tasks of community leadership. These include, not only those who help in distributing holy communion, readers in church, and catechists, but also (to use a somewhat infelicitous expression) "contact persons," i.e., laypersons who are present and accessible in parishes without a resident priest and lead the concrete life of the community to a greater or less degree, providing motivation and inspiration. Many chairpersons of parish councils carry out important leadership tasks in our communities, with great skill and complete loyalty to the priest who is responsible for the parish — and also with remarkable spiritual competence. When we hear of laypersons who lead communities in the young churches of the third world, this refers de facto to this kind of collaboration in leadership tasks under the general guidance of a parish priest.

The 1983 Code went further than this and created a completely new possibility: where there is a grave shortage of priests, it is possible for a deacon or one or several laypersons to be entrusted with the exercise of the *cura pastoralis* (canon 517 §2). In such cases, it is envisaged that specific restricted areas of jurisdiction for this community will be entrusted to a priest who is not himself the local parish priest or administrator of this community; he will exercise this authority as "moderator" in addition to his own primary field of ministry. I cannot discuss the complicated textual history of this canon, but it is clear that it is formulated in a very open manner, so that it can be applied with flexibility in various situations. For example, it does not lay down which pastoral tasks are to be entrusted to the priestly moderator; various solutions are therefore possible, depending on pastoral situations and needs. It is, however, important to note that this canon establishes a last resort (*ultima ratio*) in view of particular emergency situations; it is not intended to become de facto the normal state of affairs, nor should it be applied in such a way that the normal ecclesial structure is weakened and undermined.

Concluding Perspectives

This last danger brings us back to the ecclesiological problems mentioned at the beginning of this essay. It is clear that some attempts at a solution to the shortage of priests have side effects that dispense with the problem either by evacuating the substance of the priestly ministry or by rendering this ministry superfluous: in theory, the Catholic doctrine is retained, but in practice a parish and church structure is developed that is more or less able to do without the ordained ministry.

This danger is genuinely present when laypersons are commissioned to carry out so many of the services of the ordained ministry that we end up de facto with a structure functioning in parallel to the sacramental ministry; this problem is intensified when one layperson is entrusted with many such commissions. For example, if a pastoral assistant is commissioned — as is possible in principle, both theologically and in terms of canon law — to preach outside the eucharistic celebration, to lead worship in the absence of the priest, to baptize, to assist at marriages and to hold funerals, to take charge of community administration, etc., we end up with an official *unordained* ministry in the church. This endangers far more than the continued existence of a celibate priesthood! It puts the basic sacramental structure of the church at risk. This is why most of the German bishops are extremely reluctant to entrust pastoral assistants with the de facto leadership of parishes. The general preference is to follow the model described above and install a team of salaried or non-salaried laypersons to collaborate in specific leadership tasks; a priest will function as "moderator" of the parish by guiding this team in their service.

It would, of course, be wrong to see only dangers and deficiencies in the present situation, since it too has the potential to be what the Bible calls a *kairos*, in which the Spirit of God leads us (perhaps indeed compels us) *hominum confusione sed Dei providentia* to discover a new form of the church, of the ecclesial ministry, and of pastoral care, a form that is closer at many points to Jesus' original vision of the kingdom of God, to the *communio*-ecclesiology of Scripture and the patristic age, and to the intentions of Vatican II than the form so familiar to us from the last 150 years.

In recent years, I have visited very many parishes and have seen that the present day involves more than just the collapse of much that is old: new things too are emerging, and new forms of cooperative pastoral work are growing, showing us how a renewed form of the church might look. One of the positive things in my view is that more laypersons than in all of previous church history are involved in voluntary service in the communities, often with admirable commitment and joy. Many visits to young local churches in the so-called third world have confirmed me in this certainty.

When institutions and familiar structures break down, there is din and confusion, and the mass media are quick to come on the scene. There is no din where things are growing, and we must become sensitive to the new plants that God's Spirit cultivates before our eyes. We must encourage their growth with care. Above all, we must refuse to join in spreading the feeling that everything is going down the drain. Rather, we must diffuse a mood of encouragement, confidence, and hope, since it is well known that one can catch more flies with a single drop of honey than with a whole barrel of vinegar. I myself am one of those who remain incorrigibly convinced by the vision Pope John XXIII set out in his opening discourse at Vatican II, when he spoke of a renewed Pentecost, and I was happy to find the same perspective of hope in John Paul II's Apostolic Letter *Tertio Millennio Adveniente* in preparation for the Holy Year (1994). Let us listen with confidence to the "signs of the times" and bring the wealth of our tradition to a new splendor, in order that we may represent the person and the message of Jesus Christ credibly and convincingly, as an invitation to others, in order that the world may believe.

– 3 –

Episcopal Office

It is obvious that the ecclesiastical ministry in today's church is in crisis: the barque of Peter is in trouble at sea. This situation calls for steersmen, an image used by Paul when he includes *kubernêsis*, "the helmsman's art," in his list of the various charisms (I Cor. 12:28) and applies this term to the ministries that govern the church.[1] St. Thomas Aquinas refers in substance to this metaphor when he compares the pastors of the church to helmsmen in a storm. He is thinking here primarily (*principaliter*) of bishops.[2]

In Search of a New Vision
of the Church

It may seem a rather odd choice in our situation to turn for counsel to Thomas and his teaching on the episcopal office. After all, he lived in the feudal world of the Middle Ages, which also gave a feudal character to the bishop's ministry, thereby often obscuring its apostolic character. Besides this, we have not yet shaken off the prejudices of the liberal historians of dogma (expressed with particular clarity by A. von Harnack) who considered Thomas the father of the hierarchical and papal theory of the church.[3] Contemporary Catholic theology regards the mediaeval understanding of the episcopal office as insufficiently focused. Under the influence of Jerome, most medieval theologians followed Peter Lombard in denying that episcopal ordination was a sacrament.[4] This view was definitively superseded only by the Second Vatican Council, which taught that episcopal consecration must be understood as the plenitude of the sacrament of orders.[5] In a question such as this, it is easy to dismiss older theological works as "preconciliar," and for many people, this seems to settle the matter; but a theological genius like Aquinas is always capable of surprising the reader.

Though rooted in his own age, he differed from most of his contemporaries in his grasp of the problems posed by the historical form that the episcopal ministry had assumed at that period. At the same time, Thomas succeeded in discerning anew the original apostolic form of this ministry. This means that he proves to be the *doctor communis* in this matter as in others; he does not offer quick recipes to resolve our modern dilemmas, but he can give us sure guidance on our path.

A Time of Upheavals, a Breakthrough for the Gospel

The thirteenth century, like our own age, was a time of radical and revolutionary upheavals.[6] The immense economic restructuring entailed by the transition from an economy based on barter to one based on money was accompanied by political crises that shook the world to its very foundations, such as the struggle between the papacy and the Stauffer dynasty and the emancipation of the growing middle classes from the feudal structures dominated by the nobility and the clergy. On a deeper level, there was a far-reaching crisis within the church itself. Basic questions were posed about the institutional form of the church, inspired by the prophecies of Joachim of Fiore about the future "church of the Spirit" and by movements such as the Waldensians and Albigensians — heretical, or at least suspected of heresy — who refused to accept the rich and powerful church of the prelates and demanded a return to the simple and poor church of the apostles. Many dreamed of a church of love that would be wholly spiritual. In many cases, one motivating factor was the gnostic and Manichaean tendency to reject material reality a priori.[7]

This critique of church structures found another expression in the Franciscan and Dominican movements, which remained within the church while promoting the ideal of poverty. They called into question the parochial principle and fought for the freedom to exercise pastoral care without the material guarantees provided by church prebends. The popes in Rome took their side — often enough against the local bishops. Thus it was the poverty movements that helped the Roman claims to primacy to prevail over the episcopal structure that had characterized the church hitherto. In other words, they helped to consolidate the institution of the church in a new centralistic form.

It was not centralization that could help the church in this critical situation, however. Only a spiritual, religious renewal could help, and this was the aim of the emerging mendicant orders. M. D. Chenu is right to speak in this context of a breakthrough for the Gospel and of a movement in the spirit of the Gospel.[8] Thanks to Francis and Dominic, the Gospel acquired a new power and became the leaven of a thorough renewal that soon took hold, not only of clergy and theologians, but of the laity as a whole. This renewal was inspired by the recollection of the apostles' life in simplicity and fraternal fellowship, as they wandered from place to place, preaching and converting the people by means of their own personal testimony.

A Renewed Ecclesiological Vision

As a young scholar in Naples, in an environment open to new ideas, Thomas joined this renewal movement in the form of the Order of Preachers, which had been founded by St. Dominic. Like Francis and Dominic, Thomas, too, wanted to come to the aid of the church of his age in its difficulties. His one desire was to be a theologian of the church;[9] nevertheless, we do not find in his writings the kind of ecclesiology that developed soon after his death as a doctrine about the ecclesiastical institutions — basically, a "hierarchiology."[10] Thomas presents a completely different picture. There is no systematic treatise about the church within the framework of his theological *Summa*,[11] and this has led some scholars to speak of an ecclesiological deficit in Thomas. Such a charge is incorrect, since Thomas had a perfectly clear theological vision of the church, nourished by the spirit of the fathers and primarily spiritual in character.[12] At the same time, he had the intellectual daring to take as his starting point, not the weaknesses, but the strengths of contemporary critics of the church: his aim was to defeat them on their own ground. His entire theology was theocentric, seeking to contemplate all things *sub ratione Dei*.[13] Its structural principle is that all things proceed from God and return to him through the one mediator, Jesus Christ.[14] This makes the Gospel of Jesus Christ the Gospel of the kingdom of God, which becomes a present reality in the Holy Spirit.[15] The Holy Spirit is the heart of the church,[16] filling all the members of the church, giving them life and joining them together in unity.¹⁷ In one of the most original chapters of his theological *Summa*, dealing with the law of the Gospel, the law of the new covenant, Thomas writes that the law of the Gospel is no external law, but one inspired within us and written on our hearts; it consists of the grace of the Holy Spirit, who is bestowed on us through faith in Jesus Christ.¹⁸ This affirmation shows that Thomas is a pupil of Augustine;¹⁹ at the same time, it expresses the whole "Gospel spirit" of the Order of Preachers.²⁰ Thomas can also say that the essential element of the Christian existence, on which everything depends, is friendship and intimate communion with God.²¹ For Thomas, the mystery of the church means fellowship with God.

This spiritual perspective does not in the least lead him to dismiss the sacraments and ministries of the church as irrelevant. Certainly, Thomas does not maintain an institutional view of the church; but it is equally certain that his spiritual interpretation may not be confused with a "spiritualistic" view. His ecclesiology refuses to fall into the twin traps of institutionalization and spiritualization: instead, it has an incarnational structure.²² For Thomas, the church is based on faith and on the sacraments of faith.²³ It is above all in his scriptural commentaries that he speaks frequently of the task committed to the church and its ministries, namely, to proclaim, to teach, or (as he so often says) to evangelize.[24] The theological investigation and discussion of the sacraments are among the most important treatises in the two Summas.[25]

Nevertheless, the church's proclamation, sacraments, and ministries are not what faith and theology are really "about" — they are not ends in themselves, but are preparatory means and instruments at the service of the real matter, namely, the Christian life in and with God. At the same time, as a fruit of the reality of salvation, they have a genuine efficacy.[26] Hence, we must not misunderstand their instrumental character in a superficial manner; they are not mere external signs, but signs permeated by the Holy Spirit in such a way that they bring about in his power what they signify.[27] We can go even further: the Eucharist, the highest of all the sacraments, not only brings about but also contains what it signifies. This is why it is the center and the summit of the church's life.[28] All the other sacraments are ordered toward the Eucharist,[29] and all the ministries of the church must be understood in the light of the Eucharist and on the basis of the Eucharist.[30]

Accordingly, Thomas's vision of the church is both entirely spiritual and entirely sacramental and eucharistic. His contribution to today's ecclesiology can help us overcome the ecclesiocentric discussions within the church, which are obsessed with questions of church structure and find no way out of their dilemmas. Thomas's vision of the church is a necessary call to return to reality.

The Spiritual and Pastoral Character of the Episcopal Office

In order to understand Thomas's conception of the episcopal office correctly, we must note the point in the structure of his main theological work, the *Summa Theologiae*, where he discusses it. Naturally enough, this is in the context of sacramental doctrine, more specifically in his teaching about holy orders, although here he discusses it only as an appendix to priestly ordination.[31] His scriptural commentaries speak in greater detail of the bishops and prelates of the church. Here, as a member of the Order of Preachers, he is completely at one with the spirit of the apostle Paul: the prelates of the church are basically defined as those charged to preach.[32] They are sent to evangelize — the expression is not modern, but is found already in Thomas,[33] who offers the following pregnant summary in the *Summa*: the *officium docendi* is the *principalissimum* of the episcopal ministry.[34] He understands this "office of teaching" as the exposition of the Gospel.[35]

In the *Summa*, Thomas includes the labor of evangelization in his teaching about the perfection of the

Christian life, which consists in love *(caritas)*.³⁶ "The one who abides in love abides in God" (I John 4:16). In other words, Thomas discusses the episcopal ministry in the context of what we would call its spiritual aspect. We may find it strange that Thomas elaborates this in a tractate on the states of life in the church, where the bishops are included in the *status perfectionis*.³⁷ This, of course, does not mean that all bishops are "perfect," i.e., holy and saintly Christians. Thomas regards this as desirable, indeed highly appropriate to their office,³⁸ but he is realistic enough to know that this is not in fact always the case.³⁹ When he speaks of the *status perfectionis* of bishops, he does not mean their subjective holiness, but their objective service of sanctification. Following Dionysius's teaching about the hierarchies, Thomas holds that bishops are given the commission of *perfectores*, to accomplish the perfection and sanctification of others.⁴⁰

This starting point naturally leads to a pastoral view of the episcopal office, which is understood on the basis of the Lord's charge to Peter: "Pasture my sheep" (John 21:17).⁴¹ Thomas often cites the parable of the good shepherd who lays down his life for his sheep (John 10:11).⁴² The *principale et finale*, the main concern and ultimate goal of the bishop's office, is to be the *pastor* of the flock entrusted to his care.⁴³ The title of bishop is not honorific, but designates work to be done (*nomen operis*); *episcopus* means *superintendens*.[44] The bishop is one who exercises oversight — not in the sense of surveillance, but in vigilant concern. His precedence in rank (*praeesse*) is an existence at the service of others (*prodesse*).[45] A bishop is moved by the love of God to be the minister of others' salvation,[46] therein imitating Jesus Christ, the man for others who gives his life for the multitudes (Mark 10:45, etc.). This means that the *regimen ecclesiae* with which the bishop is charged is a pastoral service that benefits and builds up the church.[47]

The Episcopal State of Life as a Spiritual State of Life

This spiritual and pastoral approach leads to a new reflection on how the "state of life" of the bishop is to be understood. Here Thomas exercises an incomparable intellectual and theological mastery in breaking with contemporary feudal thinking about the "states" of society.

For Thomas, the state of life is connected with the person and the personal dignity of a human being: is a person free or not free, a free man or one who has been set free, a serf, a slave? In principle, this approach abandons the perspective of the feudal social order and looks rather to a free ordering based on the human rights of the person. A "state in life" is not constituted as it were naturally, thanks to one's descent; nor is it based on wealth and societal prestige, but on freedom.[48]

This is completely applicable to the states of life in the church, too, namely, the religious life and the episcopate. At his ordination, the bishop lets himself be taken in service as the pastor of the church that is entrusted to him, and he does so in a public and solemn manner.[49] For the sake of God's glory and the salvation of his flock, he must be willing to despise everything he possesses, if need be — either by giving it to the poor in his flock, or else by looking on with joy as his goods are stolen.[50] He is a successor of the apostles, and he must imitate them by accepting slander and persecution; he too must be ready to lay down his life,[51] for his ministry can lead even to martyrdom.[52] This servant character makes the episcopate more perfect than the state of life of religious. They too consecrate their lives solemnly to God, but they do so in order to be personally free for God and for communion with God, not in order to be free to be at the service of other persons' communion with God. For Thomas, active service is higher than passive behavior:[53] "Greater love has no one than he who lays down his life for his friends" (John 15:13).[54] Hence, the episcopal state and the religious life are both connected with freedom: they are generated from the very heart of what Thomas calls the *lex nova et evangelica*, which consists of the gift of the Holy Spirit, who is bestowed through faith. Since this law is internal, it is a *lex libertatis*.⁵⁵ Specifically, Christian liberty is freedom from sin and freedom for God.⁵⁶ In this liberty, the human person attains the meaning and the goal of his human freedom, namely, communion,⁵⁷ indeed friendship with God.⁵⁸ This means that the perfection of the Christian life consists in the love that is poured out into our hearts through the Holy Spirit (Rom 5:5)⁵⁹ and is the *motor, radix,* and *mater* of all the other virtues.⁶⁰ Love of God becomes visible in love of one's neighbor. It is even possible to realize the highest form of love by abandoning the contemplative life out of concern for one's neighbor: and this is the perfection appropriate to pastors of the church and to preachers.⁶¹

This spiritual and pastoral view of the episcopal office provides Thomas with the key to distinguishing it from the pastoral ministry of priests. It is not a question of listing various "powers," as if the decisive point were the distinction between what a bishop can do and a "normal" priest in the pastoral ministry cannot do. Rather, the criterion is the manner in which the bishop is charged with service, and the goal of his ministry: the *bishop* is wholly and definitively commissioned as pastor for his flock, whereas the *priest* is charged by the bishop with service in particular and limited pastoral tasks for one period of time. The priest can be dismissed from these tasks or himself give them up, and this is why the priest does not belong to the state of perfection.[62]

A "Mirror for Bishops"

This spiritual and pastoral approach leads to a kind of "mirror for bishops." Thomas does not set this out explicitly, but it is easily discerned when one notes the points of view that he finds decisively important in the debates of his own period. The point of departure and constant criterion for Thomas is the pastoral character of the bishop's office of government, following the image of the good shepherd who lays down his life for his flock.

It is interesting to note the many discussions in Thomas's works of a verse from the first Letter to Timothy: "If anyone aspires to the office of bishop, he desires a noble task" (3:1).[63] These discussions bear clear traces of negative developments that Thomas had observed in the mendicant orders themselves, and his indirect criticism of the way in which the curia made episcopal appointments[64] shows that he is enough of a realist to know about those who hunted for benefices and sold jobs. It is clear that the Letter to Timothy is not speaking of such persons, and Thomas attacks them severely, since he holds that Paul's words refer to the earliest age of the church, when acceptance of an episcopal see entailed readiness to die as a martyr. It is indeed a noble task to be willing to die like that.

On the other hand, it is wholly reprehensible to seek the episcopal office only for the sake of external advantages and honors: this is a sign of greed and pride. But Thomas also criticizes the apparently pious intention of assuming the episcopal office in order to serve others. Such service is indeed useful and praiseworthy per se, but it is a sign of presumption to seek a prominent position in order to be able to help others; according to the Letter to the Hebrews, church leaders face an especially strict judgment (13:17). A bishop must give an account before God's judgment seat of any worldly misuse of his office; he will be asked whether he has perverted his office into a worldly matter. Hence, one who strives for this office exposes himself to the risk of having to give an account of the church — and only a man with no fear of God's judgment could seriously seek such a position. This means that it is safer, with respect to the salvation of one's own soul, not to take on the office of preaching (which Thomas considers essential to the episcopal ministry).

For the sake of one's own salvation, one may accept the episcopal ministry only under obedience. Following Augustine, Thomas writes that only the necessity of love, i.e., the urgent needs of the church, provide a sufficient reason to accept this office; and these same needs forbid one to refuse the episcopal ministry when one is charged to exercise it, since a refusal would contradict both love of God and love of one's neighbor. Although the episcopal office is not necessary to anyone's salvation per se, one's salvation requires acceptance, if it is imposed upon him, and not even a vow can excuse one from this duty: the love of God means that one must care for the flock of Christ as pastor. The compelling force of love justifies abandonment of the *otium* of the contemplative life to submit to what we today would call the hectic stress of this office.[65]

In human and in Christian terms, of course, an inner serenity is required for the exercise of this exhausting ministry,[66] and this is why Thomas agrees with Augustine that the burden of pastoral office must never lead the bishop to neglect that joy in the truth that is nourished by contemplation. Thomas does not want to see bishops who are busy pastoral managers. Rather, he wants pastors who find sufficient time for study and the contemplative life not only in spite of, but precisely *because* of their pastoral concerns. Only so will they be able to do justice to the ministry of preaching that is their particular duty.[67]

The criteria governing acceptance of the episcopal office apply also to the selection of candidates. According to Thomas, piety and personal holiness cannot decide this question on their own: the decisive point is whether a man is suited to governing the church, able to instruct and defend it and rule it in peace. The goal of the episcopal office, that which gives it meaning, is the "peace of the church" (*pax ecclesiae*), unity in the variety of charisms and states of life, the building-up of the body of Christ out of many members. A bishop must not polarize, since his task is to realize the peace of the church. His is the ministry of unity and peace.

The criteria for admission are in keeping with the criteria that permit one, or even oblige one, to accept this ministry: once again, it is a question of a pastoral commission and of pastoral usefulness. This is why it is absolutely forbidden to lay down the episcopal office for the sake of personal advantages or because of external danger; not even the desire to devote oneself to the contemplative life can justify such an action. The situation is different when something prevents the exercise of the episcopal ministry — e.g., personal sins on the part of the bishop, illness, or old age. In these cases, the abandonment of the ministry may be permitted or even required. In other situations, it may be impossible for a bishop, despite his best endeavors, to continue to serve his church usefully; the best thing then is for him to look for another field of activity where he can work with greater success. In all these instances, it is the pope who has the authority to dispense the bishop from the promise he has given.[68]

This question takes on particular urgency in situations of persecution. As long as care for the salvation of those entrusted to him makes the personal presence of the bishop necessary, he must remain with his flock, and he is allowed to seek a safe refuge only if there is another to whom he can entrust his pastoral ministry. One who retreats to avoid danger, but without causing harm to his flock, is not a "hireling." But as soon as things improve, or the difficult situation requires it, he must be willing to return for the sake of the salvation of his flock.[69]

The Wealth of the Church and Care for the Poor

The test of Thomas's spiritual and pastoral vision was whether it could offer an answer to the question of poverty — the main problem of the church in his day. When his contemporaries asked about the wealth of the bishops and of the church, they were in fact putting a question mark against the entire institutional structure of the church. This wealth provoked an abundant criticism in the thirteenth century, not only among movements that were suspected of heresy or among the "Spirituals," but also among the simple people, who saw the church's wealth and therefore lent an open ear to the radical voices. More than this: the radical critics of the church seemed to find support in Jesus himself, who had sent out the seventy-two disciples with the injunction to take nothing with them, "neither purse nor bag" (Luke 10:4).[70]

Although Thomas had made his own personal decision in favor of the poverty movement, he was far from any blind radicalism. Even in this debate, which shook the church of his period to its very foundations, he remained sober and objective. It is clear that his activities at the papal court gave him sufficient insight into the complex material to enable him to form a balanced and nuanced judgment. He remained solidly planted on the soil of reality and (more importantly) of Christian doctrine.

Fundamental theological considerations led Thomas to distance himself from the radical poverty movements of his period. He holds that the total renunciation of private possessions is not a commandment, but a counsel — and hence a work of supererogation. No one is obligated to do this, unless he has bound himself by a vow of voluntary poverty. And even voluntary poverty is only an instrument: it helps to attain perfection and is a path to perfection, but it is not perfection itself.[71] This argument removes all justification for an apparent radicalism that was in fact ignorant of the world, if not in fact hostile to it. Thomas states explicitly that perfection can be compatible with wealth.[72]

The rejection of an extreme position does not of course dispose of the justified concern of the poverty movement; this first step in the argument allows Thomas to take up this concern in the correct manner, within the framework of his pastoral understanding of the episcopal office and of Christian moral and social teaching. From a pastoral perspective, he makes it clear that concern about worldly possessions must not lead the bishop to neglect the service of God. Just as God shares himself unreservedly with us, so an undivided service is expected of those who devote themselves to the service of God. General Christian social and moral teaching stipulates that the bishop is obliged to share his possessions with the poor, to whatever extent love may require. One cannot regulate down to the last penny the degree to which he is required to give aid; as with all the virtues, human prudence and one's personal conscience must avoid extremes and discern the correct measure here.[73] At any rate, we are certainly entitled to expect a bishop to exercise the virtue of generosity in a special manner.[74]

The same principles apply to ecclesiastical possessions. Thomas never says that the church is not entitled to possess anything, but he says very clearly that these possessions must be administered correctly — and here his words are merciless. He begins by observing that, according to canon law, the possessions of the church are meant not only for the poor, but also to provide for divine worship and for the servants of the church, who assuredly include the bishop. He then says unambiguously that clergy and bishops who fail to administer church goods in this way must be deposed. Thomas also applies a strict judgment to the bishop's own share in church goods: he may give his relatives and his family some part of this property if he intends to help them in their need, but not if his aim is to enrich them.

A final point is important. In situations of extreme distress, e.g., when prisoners must be ransomed or times are particularly hard, even church goods intended for worship must be given away. This applies also to the share destined for the bishop and the clergy, at least where they can supply their wants from their own private property. The same holds good of provision for the future: it is per se a matter of prudence to store up goods for the future, but in situations of grave distress, these goods too must be used to bring relief to those who are suffering.[75]

We may sum up as follows: for Thomas (unlike the "Spirituals"), the wealth of the church is not itself the problem. The central question is the correct and just administration and use of this wealth.[76] His judgment may be nuanced, but his message to his contemporaries was perfectly clear. Thomas distances himself from ideas of a spiritual church in flight from the world, since such a church would be a stranger both to the world and to the Gospel. He opts for a spiritual form of the church and of the episcopal ministry in the midst of the world — and in the midst of the world's distress. In other words, he opts for a church that administers justly, generously, and compassionately the goods that it rightly possesses. In times of need, concern for the poor must have the final word. This is not yet our modern "preferential option for the poor," but it shows how this modern option can be understood in theologically responsible terms.

The Sacramental Dimension of the Episcopal Office

This completely realistic view of the spiritual form of the church and of the episcopal office paves the ground for fundamental reflections on their institutional form. We have already seen that the church as institution cannot be an end in itself; it is only an instrument (and a fruit) of the Christian reality of salvation, which is essentially spiritual, and this provides the decisive criterion for the evaluation of the ecclesiastical institutions. When we employ this criterion, we find not only the boundaries but also the necessity and justification of the church's sacraments and ministries.

In his *Summa against the Gentiles,* Thomas gives three reasons for the necessity of the sacraments.[77] The first and most important, also adduced in the theological *Summa,*[78] is that God cares for the human person in keeping with the *conditio humana.* Since human beings are led to grasp spiritual and intellectual realities by means of things accessible to their senses, it follows that the spiritual means of salvation too must be bestowed on human persons under signs accessible to their senses.

This anthropological perspective is complemented by a second, more christological reasoning: the high point of God's salvific work in favor of the human person occurs in the incarnation of his Son. Since the incarnate Word of God is the first and comprehensive cause of salvation, the means through which we receive the salvation accomplished by Jesus Christ must possess a similarity to this cause. In these means of salvation, the divine power is at work through signs accessible to the senses.[79]

Finally, Thomas speaks of the theology of sin, a perspective that took on particular importance in view of contemporary heretical movements. The fact that a disordered attachment to earthly things led the human person to fall into sin must not be allowed to give the impression that earthly things are naturally evil. God wishes to show, by means of the sacraments, that visible realities are good, since they have been created by

God. They harm human persons only when they are attached to them in a disordered manner; but they help them attain salvation when they use them aright.

Thomas summarizes his position as follows: "This excludes the error of certain heretics who seek to remove every visible element from the sacraments of the church. Nor is this surprising, since they believe that whatever is visible is naturally evil and has an evil author."[80]

Although he highly esteems the visible order of things, Thomas refuses to see them as ends in themselves or to attribute to them a quasi-magical efficacy: in this same passage, he writes that the visible signs are merely "as it were instruments of the incarnate God." Their effect is not the result of their own natural capacities, but of their institution by Jesus Christ, and of the power of Jesus Christ at work in and through them.[81] Jesus Christ himself wishes to encounter us in them and through them.[82] In modern terms, we could call them a mediated immediacy to Jesus Christ.

The Sacramental Structure of the Ecclesiastical Ministries

Since the mediation of salvation has a sacramental structure, it follows for Thomas that this mediation also has a hierarchical structure. Under a sacramental structure, the administration of the sacraments can occur only through visible human persons; and since it is impossible for human persons to perform this ministry out of any personal competence of their own, the initiation into ecclesiastical office must itself be a sacrament that mediates grace. This sacrament bestows the spiritual power (*virtus*) necessary for the correct exercise of the ministry and empowers the minister to help build up the body of Christ without any risk to the salvation of his own soul.[83]

This line of argument is significant for two reasons. First, it indicates that the commissioning of a person for a pastoral and sacramental ministry *without* a sacramental, spiritual empowering would imperil the soul of that person by imposing on him an excessive burden; in the final analysis, therefore, such an act of commissioning is prohibited. A pastoral and sacramental task without the sacramental grace necessary to accomplish it — an "unordained ministry" — would be a law that killed, not a Gospel that set free. Second, we should note that Thomas does not justify the existence of the ecclesiastical ministries in positivistic terms. In other words, his argument does not begin with the sacramental ministry that has in fact been instituted by Jesus Christ, and then go on to ask what pastoral and sacramental tasks might be appropriate to this ministry; rather, he remains faithful to his own pastoral approach and argues on the basis of the pastoral and sacramental tasks when he seeks to justify the necessity of the sacramental ordained ministry. The ministries are not an end in themselves; they exist in order to serve. In view of many modern discussions and dilemmas, this is not merely interesting — it is immensely relevant! *Sacramenta et ministeria propter homines! Salus animarum suprema lex!* (Sacraments and ministries for human beings. The highest law is the salvation of souls).

Ultimately, all the sacraments (and in a special manner the sacrament of orders) are ordered toward the sacrament of sacraments, the Eucharist,[84] which is the greatest and the preeminent sacrament.[85] This is why the sacrament of orders must be understood primarily in relation to the Eucharist;[86] and this position leads in turn to the view that priestly ordination is primarily the empowerment to consecrate the Body and Blood of Christ. Ordination also empowers the priest to purify the people of God by means of the absolution that is necessary if reception of the Eucharist is to lead to salvation.[87]

Our initial reaction today to such a concept of the priesthood may well be to dismiss it as a sacramental reductionism; but Thomas, as a member of the Order of Preachers and a professor of theology, knows well that the sacraments must not be understood magically. Rather, they must be seen as *sacramenta fidei* and as the expression of faith (*sacramenta protestantia fidem*).[88] This means that preaching is a constitutive dimension of the correct administration of the sacraments, so that the people may be instructed about the sacraments and prepared to receive them aright. Accordingly, a priest in the pastoral ministry must be more than simply one who says the words of the Mass: he must have an adequate theological education,[89] since his ministry includes not only the power to consecrate and absolve, but the duty to preach.

Is Episcopal Ordination a Sacrament?

The concentration of the medieval theology of holy orders on the sacrament of the Eucharist left its mark on the understanding of the episcopal ministry and of episcopal ordination: since a bishop "cannot" do more than a "simple" priest with respect to the Eucharist, it was held — following Peter Lombard and appealing to the authority of Jerome — that episcopal ordination could not be a sacrament.[90]

In his commentary on the *Sentences*, Thomas agrees in principle with this view.[91] He is, however, aware of the contrary testimony of Ps.-Dionysius the Areopagite,[92] and he seeks to mediate between these two positions. This is why Thomas's own affirmations make the impression of a certain embarrassment and internal inconsistency.[93] His basic starting point is the conviction that the bishop has no higher authority with regard to the *corpus Christi verum* than the priest and, consequently, that episcopal ordination is not a specific *ordo*. He adds, however, that the bishop has a higher authority with regard to the *corpus Christi mysticum*,[94] which does allow us to speak of an *ordo* of the episcopate.[95] It is also true that, since the priest can exercise his authority only on the basis of a commission by the bishop and within the framework of the *corpus Christi mysticum*, which it is the bishop's task to regulate, he does not possess his sacramental authority in an autonomous manner; rather, he shares in the authority of the bishop.[96]

Thomas frequently describes the distinction between the bishop and the simple priest with regard to the *corpus Christi mysticum*.[97] This concerns all serious matters that are of fundamental importance for the church,[98] especially those that constitute the presupposition for a legitimate celebration of the Eucharist — not only priestly ordination, but the consecration of altars and sacred vessels.[99] Thomas also mentions the administration of confirmation, the consecration of virgins, the consecration of chrism, and the holding of synods.[100] Because of the bishop's responsibility for the body of Christ, i.e., the church, Thomas demands that he have a deeper knowledge of the faith than can be required of priests.[101]

Thomas's thinking on this question did not remain static: his study of the biblical testimony and of the richer tradition of the church, which differed from Peter Lombard, helped Thomas develop his ideas, and it is in fact typical of his theology of the episcopal office that he proceeds, not by means of a priori deductions, but on the basis of the positive testimony of Scripture and tradition. He offers a biblical justification of the distinction between bishops and priests by tracing the bishops back to the vocation of the twelve apostles and the priests to the sending out of the seventy-two other disciples (Luke 10:1). He is also aware of the developments in the history of theology. He states that the concepts of "bishops" (*episkopoi*) and "priests" (*presbuteroi*) were originally used synonymously; although there were substantial differences in the contents of these two ministries, a clearer differentiation became necessary only in order to resist schismatic tendencies.[102] He notes the importance attached in the New Testament epistles to the laying on of hands when the episcopal ministry is handed on; Thomas holds that this involves not only the commissioning for a ministry, but the transmission of a grace.[103] A number of testimonies from the church's tradition confirm him in this view.[104] This is why Thomas rejects as heretical the view of Aërius[105] that there is no distinction between priest and bishop.[106]

This leads Thomas in his later works to offer a more nuanced answer to the question of the sacramentality of episcopal ordination. A key role is played here by the Opusculum *De perfectione vitae spiritualis*,[107] where Thomas makes the same distinction as in the Supplement to his *Summa Theologiae:* although the bishop does not possess more authority with regard to the *corpus Christi verum* in the Eucharist than the "simple" priest, he does possess a higher authority with regard to the *corpus Christi mysticum* (i.e., the church), and from this perspective one may speak of an *ordo*.[108] Thomas can also say: *episcopatus enim non est novus ordo, sed gradus in ordine* (The episcopate is not a new order but a rank in order).[109]

The significance of these affirmations becomes clear when we consider the connection that Thomas makes between the eucharistic *corpus Christi verum* and the ecclesial *corpus Christi mysticum*. The true, bodily presence of Christ in the sacrament is not the real goal, the real matter with which this sacrament is concerned (*res sacramenti*); this is only an intermediate reality (*res et sacramentum*) that points us symbolically and causally to the real matter, namely, the upbuilding of the mystical body of the Lord.[110] Since the episcopal office is antecedent and superior to that of the priest with regard to this upbuilding of the church, it is ordered in a particular way to the "real concern" of the Eucharist. As Ignatius of Antioch ruled, as early as the second century, every celebration of the Eucharist must occur in fellowship with the bishop.[111] Not all the obscurities are cleared up, and some inconsistencies remain;[112] nevertheless, in terms of the history of theology, Thomas succeeded in elaborating a conception with a broader historical significance than he himself could have completely grasped. Other masters of scholastic theology before him had posited a relationship between the *corpus Christi verum* and the *corpus Christi mysticum*,[113] but a comparison with Bonaventure's commentary on the Sentences shows that the consequences that Thomas draws from this relationship in his own commentary on the Sentences, and even more clearly in his later works, for the understanding of the episcopal ministry were certainly not something taken for granted by his contemporaries.[114]

He took at least the first step toward healing the breach that had arisen, as a result of the first and second eucharistic controversies, between the sacramental and mystical reality of the church on the one hand and its institutional, hierarchical form on the other.[115] Thanks to this breach, the church in its external form came more and more to seem a purely sociological reality, a mere apparatus of power. Thomas's theological conception broke through the boundaries of his own age, laying the foundations for a renewal in ecclesiology and sacramental theology that unfortunately came only much later on.[116]

Primacy and Episcopacy

Thomas's sacramental vision of the church also determines his definition of the relationship between primacy and episcopacy — another question that was prominent in his age, in connection with the debate about poverty, since the new mendicant orders were supported by the pope in their controversies with the secular clergy. (As mentioned above, this was an important factor in strengthening Roman primatial authority.)[117]

Thomas, who himself worked at the papal court for a long period, often emphasizes the necessity of the universal authority of the pope, basing this biblically on the New Testament texts about Peter (Matt. 16:18; Luke 22:32; John 21:15–17) and speculatively on the necessity of such an authority for the unity of the church.[118] These arguments led him to follow the tradition since Gregory VII and Innocent III[119] and teach the *plenitudo potestatis* of the pope,[120] who takes within the church the place of Christ, the Head of the church.[121] This means that he is entrusted with the care of the universal church;[122] he is *episcoporum summus*,[123] *primus et maximus omnium episcoporum* (the highest of the bishops, the first and greatest of all the bishops).[124] He has the authority to make doctrinal decisions on questions of the faith.[125]

Such an understanding of the primatial authority of the pope does not make Thomas the initiator of this doctrine (as is sometimes asserted, either praising him or blaming him); nor is he an extreme representative of this teaching. Here we should note the difference between the descriptions of the pope's position in Thomas and Bonaventure. It was the latter theologian (not Thomas) who was the most important theoretician of the papal monarchy in the thirteenth century.[126] For Bonaventure, the pope is the primary source, point of departure and regulatory factor for all ecclesiastical ministries, the summit from which power flows down in a well-ordered descent to the lowest members of the church.[127] We look in vain for such a papalist view in Thomas, who does not consider the pope the *fons et origo* of the bishops' authority; for Aquinas, all the pope does is to assign the bishops their authority and to regulate its exercise.[128] He is the guarantor of unity; but the spiritual authority itself is received by the bishop through his consecration.[129] From a sacramental point of view, the pope has no more authority than any other bishop: with regard to the *ordo episcopalis*, all bishops are equal.[130]

Thomas does not see the church as one huge diocese with the pope as a super-bishop who absorbs the authority of the individual bishops. Accordingly, in the controversy about the mendicants, he does not appeal directly to the universal jurisdiction of the pope, but respects the specific responsibility of the local bishops who occupy the place of our Lord Jesus Christ in the church.[131]

The Meaning and the Boundaries of Spiritual-Sacramental Authority

Aquinas's concept necessarily entailed consequences for his understanding of spiritual power and authority in general. He had to meet the objection that the claims made on behalf of such a *potestas* contradicted Christian freedom, perverting the church into an authoritarian system that suppressed human (and Christian) freedom.[132] This objection was to recur often, both in the Reformation period and in the modern age. Thomas takes it very seriously, since he regards the *lex nova* as a *lex libertatis*. It follows that every ecclesiastical authority must have what we today would call a liberating character.

Thomas responds to this objection by returning to his primary concern, which is pastoral. He affirms that authority deprives people of their freedom only when it seeks to promote its own interests; it sets people free when its aim is the good of the other person. Even today, we tend to understand power as the ability to impose one's own view, one's will and interests on others, thanks to one's position in society. The Gospel says that there should be no such "lords" and "slaves" among Christians (Mark 10:43); but according to the will of

Jesus Christ, there does exist an authority that is exercised, not for one's own benefit, but for the benefit and the salvation of others. This authority is concerned with other people's salvation. The *praeeminentia* that is a characteristic of authority[133] is a spiritual and pastoral service: *praeesse*, "being at the head," means *prodesse*, "being at the service" of others.[134] Finally, the *regimen ecclesiae* means that the bishop, as visible head of his church,[135] acts publicly in the name of the church[136] and is the servant of the church's peace and unity.[137]

No human being can attribute such spiritual authority to himself, still less is it a power that one might seize for oneself — one must receive the empowerment to exercise it, and this takes place through the sacramental character conferred by the sacrament of ordination,[138] which configures the ordinand to the unique high priest Jesus Christ, whose whole existence is for others. Accordingly, spiritual authority cannot be exercised in one's own name, but only in the name and in the person of Jesus Christ.[139] In the *repraesentatio Christi*, the bishop is to shape his church in keeping with the image of Jesus Christ;[140] this requires him to offer himself to Jesus Christ as an instrument, since Jesus Christ himself is the Head of his body, the church,[141] and is the primary celebrant of the sacraments.[142] Even in the mediation of the sacraments, salvation is ultimately bestowed on us through the personal encounter with Jesus Christ.[143]

When he exercises his authority, therefore, it ceases to belong to the ecclesial minister himself, since its basic reality is to point beyond him to Jesus Christ.

This authority is an essential dimension of the Christian order of salvation, since no one can redeem himself. We all depend on redemption "from outside" and "from above."[144] The church's ministry represents this salvation "from outside" and "from above," reminding the human person that salvation is a gift he receives, not a task that would place an intolerable burden on him. Spiritual authority is a sign that makes it clear that the reality of Christian salvation is gift and grace; though, to be precise, this authority does not mediate salvation itself, but only the means of salvation, namely, the sacraments.[145] It shows that God wishes to be close to us in Jesus Christ in a human manner, through other human beings, for the sake of our salvation.

This line of argument also reveals the boundaries of spiritual authority — the same Jesus Christ who is the foundation of spiritual authority has also set limitations upon it. The authority of the church's ministry reaches only as far as the Gospel — hence, we may say that we do not believe in the church, but in God; we believe in the church only to the extent that it proclaims the word of God.[146] We follow church leaders only to the extent that they themselves follow Christ.[147] This is why Thomas warns the pastors of the church not to contradict Christian freedom by turning the Gospel, which is a law of freedom, into an oppressive, burdensome human law.[148] Some situations oblige one to obey God and one's conscience rather than the leaders of the church.[149] Indeed, one may even be obliged to accept excommunication rather than act against one's own conscience.[150]

We see the seriousness with which Thomas takes the freedom of the Gospel above all in an article in his *Summa Theologiae* that is completely without parallel in the theology of his age. Thomas asks here not only whether and how Jesus Christ is the head of the church, but also whether and how he is the head of all human persons,[151] and his answer is surprising. He recognizes not only a fellowship with Jesus Christ on the basis of faith, but also a fellowship on the basis of love: wherever love is found, Jesus Christ is present and salvation becomes a reality — even without and outside the institution of the church and its sacraments.

The Beauty of the Church and the Promise Made to the Episcopal Office

Despite its limitations and risks, the episcopal ministry has a splendor of its own in Thomas's eyes. By building up the body of Christ out of many members, it serves peace in the church. The internal and external beauty of the church consists of a well-ordered unity in multiplicity, and Thomas never tires of speaking of this beauty, which profoundly fascinates him.[152]

Neoplatonic ideas (mediated to Thomas above all by Ps.-Dionysius the Areopagite) undoubtedly play a decisive role in this vision of the church, but ultimately, for Thomas as for Augustine in the *City of God*,[153] it involves the eschatological dimension of the church, which includes both the *ecclesia coelestis* and the *ecclesia in statu viae*. These are two different states of existence of one and the same church.[154] Thomas argues (against the progressive conception of salvation history in Joachim of Fiore) that the time of the church is the "last days."[155] Jesus Christ has instituted the church to last until the end of time; the heavenly Jerusalem is already descending upon the earth in the church,[156] and the kingdom of God is already present in the church.[157]

This eschatological dimension belongs to the sacramental structure of the church, for Thomas sees the sacraments as *signa prognostica* of the world to come.[158] In particular, the Eucharist is an anticipatory image and foretaste of heaven and of the bliss that awaits us in the heavenly Jerusalem.[159] The apostolic office too shares in this eschatological dimension and is to last until the end of the world (Matt. 28:20).[160] The *pax ecclesiae* that the bishop's spiritual authority is meant to serve is a fruit of the Holy Spirit[161] and a proleptic image of the eschatological peace that it makes present.[162]

Thus, Thomas does not only see the church and its episcopal office in terms of storms and struggles; ultimately, he also sees it in the context of the eschatological promise. As the episcopal ring visibly shows, the bishop is not only the storm-tossed helmsman. He is also the *sponsus*, the "bridegroom" of the church,[163] whose liturgy is the anticipated celebration, indeed the presence of the heavenly wedding feast. This is why the proper reaction is not fear and panic, but the serenity born of faith.[164] This inner calm is possible when we are certain that he whom even wind and sea obey is with us in the boat (Mark 4:41).

– 4 –

The Apostolic Succession
An Ecumenical Problem

The Problem

Results of the discussions of the ecumenical working party on the mutual condemnations of the sixteenth century bear impressive testimony to the fact that over the last two decades many controversies of the past have been resolved or at least the parties have come closer to agreement. This applies *inter alia* to questions about church ministry, which, however, continues to be regarded as the crux of ecumenical dialogue. Cardinal Joseph Ratzinger has gone so far as to call "tradition and apostolic succession" the "core question in the Catholic/Protestant debate."[1] Accordingly, the broad consensus that has been attained on the sacramentality of ministry will lead further only when we can agree about the apostolic succession in the ministry.[2] Despite a number of noteworthy new perspectives, however, no full consensus exists on this question.[3] The question of church primacy,[4] likewise far from resolved, is a partial aspect of this more general problem, which it presents in concentrated form.

There can be no doubt that the various partners have come closer to one another on the question of succession, and that mutual understanding has grown. The creed that all the churches share professes belief in the one *ecclesia apostolica*, and all agree that the apostolic testimony remains normative for every age; it is when we ask what "apostolicity" means that the churches part company. The first Plenary Assembly of the Ecumenical Council of Churches in Amsterdam (1948) regarded the emphasis on the visible "horizontal" continuity of the church in the apostolic succession of the episcopal office as the most profound difference between the basic positions taken by Catholics and Protestants; the latter place the primary emphasis on the "vertical" initiative taken by the Word of God and the response made by faith.[5] A considerably different note is sounded in many ecumenical papers published since then, especially in the Lima documents. Even the churches of the Reformation are willing today under certain conditions "to accept episcopal succession as a sign of the apostolicity of the life of the church as a whole."[6]

Why does the problem of the apostolic succession, in the sense of apostolic succession in the episcopal ministry, continue to present difficulties? One factor is certainly the confrontation between two institutional church structures that have pursued different historical developments, creating a conflict that theological interpretations on their own cannot resolve. In the last analysis, this question involves the theological significance of history and of institutions themselves: in other words, the issue of apostolic succession touches the most basic structure of the church. The Lutheran/Catholic document on "church fellowship in word and sacrament" (which has not received the attention it deserves) points out that the confessions make essentially different definitions of the relationship between the visible institutional form and the hidden spiritual essence of the church, which only faith can perceive. "The church fellowship that broke off in the sixteenth century cannot be reestablished, unless this controversial question can be resolved."[7]

Even in the sixteenth century, the various controversial positions were based on different ecclesiologies. Up to now, however, ecclesiology has not been an explicit theme of ecumenical documents in general or of the debates about lifting the anathemas of the past.[8] Discussion of the mutual recognition of ministries has usually been far too brief, and the dilemmas we face in today's ecumenical dialogue are the logical outcome of this situation.

In this essay, I shall attempt to move the question of ministry out of its narrow confines and to indicate a helpful path for future discussions on the basis of the fruits of previous ecumenical dialogue. We must, however, begin by recalling briefly the scriptural and patristic foundations in order to grasp that the root of our common dilemma lies in displacements of emphasis that had diminished the understanding of the ecclesial structure as a whole long before the sixteenth century.

Biblical Foundations of the Apostolic Succession

The biblical foundations of the apostolate and of the apostolic succession seemed clear and certain until the advent of historical-critical exegesis: it was Jesus himself who installed the twelve in office as his apostles, and after the traitor Judas had abandoned his ministry, they elected Matthias to take his place and then governed the post-Easter church, with the help of Paul at a later stage as apostle of the Gentiles. This consensus has been thoroughly shattered by modern exegesis, but no new historical reconstruction has found universal agreement among scholars.[9]

There is at any rate virtually full agreement that the starting point and criterion of the apostolic office are the call and mission imparted by the risen Lord (Gal. 1:1, 12, 16; 1 Cor. 9:1; 15:9f.; Rom. 1:5f.). This means that the apostolic office is unique: "The apostolic proclamation has its place in the event of the revelation of Christ as that particular form of proclamation that the revelation gave itself."[10] This makes the apostolic testimony the abiding foundation of the later church (Eph. 2:20). When we look at the details, however, it is clear that the apostolic office was structured in a variety of ways. The distinction between the apostolic circle in Jerusalem and Paul was not so important here as is often suggested, for Paul himself often links his own apostolate to the Jerusalem apostles (1 Cor. 15:8–11; Gal. 1:17), and he attaches great importance to his fellowship with them (Acts 15; Gal. 2). More important is the distinction between the first apostles and the charismatic wandering apostles (see Acts 13:1–3; 14:4, 14; Didache 10–15) or the apostles in the local communities (Phil. 2:25; 2 Cor. 8:23; perhaps also Rom. 16:7). Obviously, these ministries (and many others) did not owe their existence to the primal apostolic office, nor were they specific articulations of that ministry: they were charisms immediately bestowed by the Spirit and acknowledged both by the community and by Paul (Rom. 12:6–8; 1 Cor. 12:28).

Besides this, the New Testament acknowledges the transmission of apostolic offices. Acts 6 attests that the apostles conferred office on a college of seven men at an early date. According to Acts 15, the presbyters in Jerusalem participate in the decision made by the apostles at the so-called apostolic council. In Paul's farewell discourse at Miletus (Acts 20:17–38), he speaks of presbyters or bishops who have been appointed as shepherds by the Spirit of God, with the task of caring for the flock "after my departure" (v. 28f.). In other words, they are to perform the tasks that he has performed up to that date. The Pastoral Letters, written by a disciple of Paul, give the clearest testimony, when they exhort Timothy and Titus to install suitable office-bearers with prayer and the laying on of hands (1 Tim. 4:14; 2 Tim. 1:6; Titus 1:5; see also Acts 14:23). Here we already have a transmission of ministry, indeed a chain of office-bearers, which goes from Paul, via his disciple who wrote the Pastoral Letters, to Timothy and Titus, and finally reaches the new office-bearers who are to receive the ministry at their hands.

This allows us to see the transition from the apostolic to the postapostolic age within the New Testament itself. Although it is impossible for the apostles to have successors in their unique apostolic office, this ministry involves preaching and the foundation and government of churches, and these tasks must continue in the church. Accordingly, the unique office of the apostles must be distinguished from the continuing apostolic office, which is tied to the unique office of the apostles and remains necessary for the church.

These apostolic offices, which already existed during the apostles' lifetime but emerged more clearly after their deaths, are not understood in the New Testament as a merely human institution, but as spiritual charisms created and bestowed by the Holy Spirit (Acts 20:28). This is why, as we have seen, they are conferred with prayer and the laying on of hands. According to the summary in Ephesians 4:10–12, these ministries are a gift from heaven, bestowed by the exalted Lord himself on the church to build it up. The main accent lies not on the "horizontal" transmission of the ministry from one office-bearer to his successor, but on the "vertical" act of empowerment by the exalted Lord in the Holy Spirit. There is thus no antithesis between office and charism; although of course they are not identical, they are closely connected.

The missionary charge that the risen Lord imparts at the close of the synoptic Gospels and at the beginning of Acts (Matt. 28:20; see also Mark 16:15; Luke 24:47f.; Acts 1:8) points in the same direction and reveals another dimension of succession in the apostolic office. This charge is based on a universal christology with eschatological claims: "All authority has been given to me in heaven and on earth.... I am with you always, to the close of the age." The apostles are commanded to bear witness to the Gospel of Jesus Christ before all peoples and in all ages. In other words, their mission extends beyond the lifetime of the first witnesses, and this means that after the death of the first (and primary) witnesses there must be others who will take on this mission and continue it. This is not a succession in the linear sense, where one office-bearer follows another; rather, new members are coopted and integrated into the apostolic college with its mission that is carried on from age to age.

Here we have another decisive aspect of the apostolic succession: it does not exist for its own sake, but is completely at the service of the Gospel of Jesus Christ, whose norms it observes. As the introduction to Romans shows, Paul's apostolate is completely concerned with the proclamation of the Gospel (Rom. 1:1–6), and his goal is to give it concrete form in the church not only by means of words, but also through the apostle's entire existence (1 Cor. 4:10–16; 2 Cor. 4:7–10). The apostle understands himself as a model for his communities (Phil. 3:17; Titus 2:7; 1 Pet. 5:3). Accordingly, the apostolic succession is never a mere institutional matter; it must also be understood in existential terms, as a following of the apostles' teaching and life.

This is why Paul becomes the prototype of ecclesial ministry in the later New Testament writings. The Pastoral Letters also link this ministry to the "deposit" of the faith (*parathêkê*) that has been handed down (1 Tim. 6:20; 2 Tim. 1:12, 14). The apostolic succession is a sign and a testimony, in the threefold sense summarized in a well-known passage of Thomas Aquinas:[11] as *signum rememorativum*, it is to recall and point backward to the Gospel of Jesus Christ, which was handed on once and for all by the apostles; as *signum demonstrativum*, it is to make the inherited Gospel present here and now as a living authority; as *signum prognosticum*, it is to be a prophetic sign and testimony that anticipates the definitive kingdom of God.[12]

In biblical terms, the reality later called "apostolic succession" can be understood aright only in the total context of christology, pneumatology, ecclesiology, and eschatology. It is the concrete form in which and through which Jesus Christ remains with us in the Holy Spirit until the end of time.[13] It is the concrete form of the *pro nobis* that occurred once and for all.[14] Jesus Christ's handing over of himself remains present in the handing on of the apostolic tradition, in which and through which he continually hands himself over to us so that he may remain with us always.[15]

Apostolic Succession in the Early Church as the Framework for a Future Consensus

The apostolic succession is attested de facto in the New Testament, though it is not the object of specific theological consideration there. As the early church reflected on this theme, trajectories already indicated in Scripture were drawn more clearly in the second-century debates with gnosis, which presented a threat to the most basic structures of the church — but at the same impelled the church to become conscious of these structures.[16]

After the initial stages in the Pastoral Letters, I Clement, Hegesippus, etc., this becomes especially clear in Irenaeus of Lyons and Tertullian. Irenaeus's debate with the gnostics concerned "the only true and life-giving faith, which the church has received from the apostles and imparts to her children."[17] Christ gave the apostles the commission to proclaim the Gospel, and their preaching and writings were to be "the foundation and bulwark of our faith." The apostolic origin is transmitted by the Holy Spirit; the apostles themselves received the fullness of knowledge from the Spirit,[18] who handed this truth over to the church and inscribed it upon the hearts of the faithful.[19] Thus anyone who wants to see the truth can find the tradition proclaimed by the apostles in every local church. Within the church, the tradition is attested and preserved by those who were installed by the apostles as bishops of the individual churches and by their successors.[20] In concrete terms, then, the tradition has come to us in the order of bishops and their succession;[21] they have received the sure charism of truth[22] and represent in a personal, charismatic manner the substance of faith delivered to the church. It is their task to preserve and actualize this faith. It follows that the apostolic succession is the concrete sign that allows us to recognize the tradition and indeed the body of Christ.[23]

The apostolic succession is completely at the service of the apostolic tradition. This is why ordination to the episcopal office was linked at a very early date to the profession of the creed.[24] We find the apostolic tradition only in the mode of apostolic succession, and the normative substance of this concrete form is the tradition itself.[25] This link between the apostolic tradition and the succession is the consequence of understanding the church and its ministries as a sacrament, i.e., a sign and instrument of salvation: succession in the ministry is understood as a sign and instrument of the *res*, namely, the transmission of the Gospel. Apostolicity in the sense of historical continuity serves to ensure apostolicity in the sense of the substantial identity of the apostolic message.

This means that *successio* cannot be detached from *traditio*. But it is also inseparable from *communio*, as we see in the collaboration of the community in the appointment of its bishop, in the requirement that a new bishop should be ordained by at least three consecrating bishops,[26] and in the "letters of communion" that the new bishop received from his fellow bishops. Since all the bishops who are in the line of apostolic succession share in the one mission in the one Spirit, they form together the one *ordo episcoporum*,[27] in Cyprian's words, *episcopatus unus atque indivisus* (the episcopate is one and undivided).[28] Augustine formulates the rule: *quod universa tenet ecclesia, nec conciliis institutum, sed semper retentum est, non nisi auctoritate apostolica traditum rectissime creditur* (what is held by the whole church, and not as instituted by councils, but as a matter of invariable custom, is rightly held to have been handed down by apostolic authority).[29] When a bishop enters the apostolic succession, he does not receive some private channel (or "pipeline") connecting him to the apostles. Rather, he enters the fellowship of bishops. The individual bishop is a successor of the apostles, not thanks to an unbroken chain going back from his predecessors to one of the apostles, but because he is in communion with the entire *ordo episcoporum*, which as a whole is the successor of the apostolic college and of the apostles' mission.[30] This is why the mutual agreement of the bishops is a decisive sign of the apostolicity of their teaching. Catholicity is an instrument and expression of apostolicity.[31]

This link between *traditio*, *successio*, and *communio* does not lead to a mechanical automatism. *Successio* is a sign of the true *traditio*, but not its guarantee.[32] One bishop, or several, can also deny the *traditio* and thus fall away from *communio*. In this situation, one must refuse to obey them: this is the unanimous teaching from Irenaeus[33] and Augustine[34] to Thomas Aquinas.[35] This is why the history of the early and the medieval church knows many instances of depositions and condemnations of bishops and even of popes,[36] of synods that taught heresy and therefore were not received as authentic, and of periods when it was not the bishops but the lay faithful who handed on the true faith.[37] This means that the sign of *successio* does not invariably guarantee the *res*, i.e., the true *traditio*. The church and its theology took longer to perceive that the *res* — the Spirit who guarantees the true *traditio* — can be present even where the sign (whether *successio* or *communio*) is for some reason absent or not fully existent; the excessive authority attributed to Augustine on this question was definitively corrected only by Vatican II.[38] We do, however, find this lapidary formulation in Thomas Aquinas: "God has not bound his power to the sacraments in such a way that it would be impossible for him to communicate the effect of the sacraments without the sacraments themselves."[39]

In specific cases, it is certainly possible for the *successio*, understood as a sign, to part company with the *res* that it designates and attests, namely, the *traditio*; there are no automatic guarantees here. But one should not turn exceptional situations into the normal case; rather, one should adopt the patristic view that *traditio*, *successio*, and *communio* are essentially interrelated. With its basically holistic conception and its openness and elasticity, the tradition of the early church offers a helpful framework for understanding isolated later developments. One important contribution to the unity of the divided churches is reflection on the common patrimony represented by this tradition.

The Divergence of Tradition and Succession in the Middle Ages and in the Reformation

The Middle Ages lost any clear awareness of the inherent connection between *traditio*, *successio*, and *communio*. The reasons were numerous, and the development complicated; we cannot discuss this in detail here. The decisive event was the disappearance of the patristic sacramental ecclesiology in the aftermath of the second eucharistic controversy in the eleventh century.[40] From now on, the church was increasingly understood only as a legal structure, where ministerial authority was no longer a sacramental *repraesentatio* brought about by the Spirit, but a *potestas* bestowed on the individual office-holder as his personal possession.[41] In the framework of a system of absolute ordination (i.e., detached from service of a concrete local church), this *potestas* was no longer thought of as necessarily related to *communio*. This meant that the *ordo* became an isolated sacramental rite of ordination, the sacrament of priestly ordination, while ordination to the episcopal office was mostly seen, not as sacramental, but as conferring a greater measure of *potestas* (or *iurisdictio*) and *dignitas* in the church than that possessed by "simple" priests.[42]

This explains why jurisdictional acts of late medieval popes could give some nonbishops (i.e., "simple priests") the authority to ordain.[43] The papal authorization preserved in principle the connection of such ordinations with the *ordo episcoporum*. This means that the so-called presbyteral succession is neither a substitute nor an alternative to episcopal succession: rather, it is one form of the episcopal succession.[44] We see the problematic consequences of the restricted medieval perspective in the fact that a whole sequence of archbishops in Cologne in the sixteenth century never received episcopal ordination; this is no isolated occurrence. The inherent link between *successio, traditio*, and *ordinatio* had been lost to sight, and this was one of the numerous deplorable factors that prevented many from experiencing the church in its external form as a sign of salvation and truth. The face of the church had been too profoundly disfigured.

If one wishes to understand why the Reformers criticized the church and ecclesiastical office so sharply, one must be aware of this background.[45] They criticized an ordained priesthood that was understood in a one-sided and narrowly sacramental manner, often completely detached from the preaching of the Word and service of the community; they also protested against an episcopal and papal ministry that was experienced as an alien tyranny. Nevertheless, the Reformers did not intend to break the connection with the episcopal ministry in its historical succession, provided only that the bishops were "right bishops" who permitted them to preach in accordance with the Gospel (understood in the light of the Reformation doctrine of justification). When no bishops proved willing to embrace the Reformation and appoint office-bearers for those parishes that had accepted the new teaching, the Reformers themselves appointed their own ministers. This was explicitly described as an emergency measure. They appealed to Jerome for support of their claim that there was no fundamental difference between the ministry of a parish priest and that of a bishop; they were also convinced that apostolicity was an attribute of the church as a whole, which consequently had the right to appoint its own office-bearers.[46]

The latter justification of the ordinations carried out by the Reformers[47] makes it difficult to accept the thesis that their criticism was directed only against abuses and corruptions and that they continued to view their own ecclesiology merely as an interim solution forced upon them by external circumstances. Their starting point in the divergence they experienced between the original Gospel and the de facto state of the church led them to emphasize the freedom and superiority of the Gospel vis-à-vis the de facto church. This "polarity" between Gospel and church encouraged them to trust that the Gospel itself would prevail in the power of the Holy Spirit and that it would be heard: this does not require any link to particular offices or persons.[48] Hence, the true *successio* lies in the Gospel itself.[49]

This made the question of continuity with an office in presbyteral or episcopal succession a matter of purely human law. This appears to dismantle the inherent connection between *traditio* and *successio*, between the Gospel and the concrete church (which was essential for the early church), not only in individual cases but in principle. This position has been maintained consistently and is found in the most recent ecumenical convergence documents, which acknowledge the apostolic succession in the episcopal office as desirable and recommendable, but not as theologically indispensable.[50]

This decision by the Reformers concerns not one isolated partial problem, but the total sacramental view of the church, i.e., the question whether the church's visible elements are sacraments and signs of its spiritual essence, which can be perceived only in faith. It is true that the Reformers did not understand the hiddenness of the church in the sense of a *civitas platonica*.[51] Unlike the enthusiastic groups, they clearly recognized in word and sacrament, and in ecclesial ministries, visible elements *in* the church.⁵² But this does not amount to the affirmation that the salvation bestowed by God once and for all is mediated *through* the church.⁵³ Accordingly, the primary break was not caused by an interruption of the chain of succession, but by a new understanding of the relationship between the church and the Gospel of salvation in Jesus Christ.⁵⁴ F. Schleiermacher may have exaggerated this point, but his formulation of the difference points in the right direction, when he said that Protestantism "makes the relationship of the individual to the church dependent on his relationship to Christ," while Catholicism "makes the relationship of the individual to Christ dependent on his relationship to the church."⁵⁵ One must of course ask whether this Protestant position is merely the fruit of an emergency situation that has lasted to the present day, or whether the emergency regulation established in the sixteenth century has a foundational and constitutive character; contemporary Protestantism appears to answer this question in a variety of ways.

It was difficult for the Council of Trent to find a satisfactory response,⁵⁶ partly because Catholic theology at that period no longer fully recalled the sacramental ecclesiology that had posited an inherent connection between *traditio* and *successio,* and partly because the Reformation posed the question of tradition and succession in a new manner. In its fourth session, the council affirmed the connection between the Gospel and the church, and between Scripture and tradition, and the obligatory character of the church's exposition of Scripture.[57] When it set out the doctrine of the sacrament of orders, Trent rejected several exaggerated formulations of the Reformation understanding of ministry, maintaining the apostolic succession of the bishops and their superiority to presbyters.[58] This preserved the core of the patristic conception of the church with its episcopal structure as location, sign, and instrument of the Gospel, but the inherent sacramental connection was no longer clear. Besides this, the Reformers' questioning of the external juridical structure of the church and of the ecclesial mediation of salvation led in the course of the Counter-Reformation to a juridical narrowness that was alien to the early and the medieval church.[59]

We see the extent to which Trent thought in legal categories when we consider the council's evaluation of ordination in the Protestant churches: ministers who have not been ordained or commissioned correctly (*rite*) by the ecclesiastical and canonical authority (*potestas*) are called illegitimate ministers of the word and the sacraments.[60] The question of succession was understood here as a question of the legitimacy of ministry, not as a matter of the sacramentality of the church. This narrow perspective had at least the positive virtue (from a modern point of view) of allowing a certain degree of openness and flexibility in the question of recognizing the ministries that exist in the churches of the Reformation, since the affirmation that ministries "seized by the ministers' own presumption" are illegitimate[61] does not entail an explicit judgment about the validity or invalidity of ministries conferred in a manner that the separated churches themselves consider legitimate.[62] This question can be resolved only in a larger theological context, i.e., within a renewed sacramental understanding of the church.

Convergences since the Second Vatican Council — and the Difference That Remains

Building on previous theological study of this topic, the Second Vatican Council[63] achieved a renewal of the sacramental vision of the church as a complex reality consisting both of human, visible, and institutional elements and of a spiritual and divine element that can be grasped only by faith (*Lumen Gentium* 8). Protestant theology too has reflected on the sacramental structure of the church.[64]

Within this total sacramental vision of the church, the council teaches that episcopal ordination is a sacrament[65] and clearly sets out the inherent connection between *successio*, *traditio*, and *communio*.[66] While the formulation in the constitution on the church might still give the impression of a one-sidedly linear understanding of the apostolic succession as an unbroken continuity in office, the constitution on revelation emphasizes the connection between the mission of the apostles and the assistance of the Holy Spirit that they are promised, between the believing church as a whole and the Holy Spirit, and between the apostolic succession and guidance by the Spirit of truth.[67] This pneumatological conception comes fully into its own in the decree on missionary activity:[68] the continuity between Christ and the church is mediated by the Holy Spirit, who sustains, accompanies, and guides its apostolic activity, sometimes indeed going ahead of it.[69] After all the narrow restrictions of the past, the council succeeded in presenting anew in unambiguous terms the broad pneumatological and ecclesiological context of the apostolic succession. This repristination of the holistic conception of the early church created a better framework for ecumenical dialogue about the ministry and ministerial succession.

Two points show how elastic the conciliar framework is, and how it succeeds in doing justice to the nuances revealed by historical study of this question. First, the council merely states that, among the various ministerial offices, the episcopal office has had a preeminent place from earliest times, so that the bishops share their ministry with priests and deacons.[70] It does not assert that the threefold hierarchical articulation into the episcopal, priestly, and diaconal ministries was instituted directly by God, but only affirms that the one ministry has been exercised in this threefold manner *ab antiquo*, "from early times."[71] These open formulations take account of a number of historical problems and go some way toward meeting the positions of the Reformers with respect to the original equality of the presbyteral and the episcopal office. Catholic theology, too, sees several open questions here.

Second, the council consciously avoids saying that only bishops can receive new members into the college of bishops; it refrains from deciding the *quaestio iuris* and the *quaestio facti* on this issue and merely makes the positive affirmation: "It is the right of bishops to admit newly elected members into the episcopal body by means of the sacrament of Orders."[72] This at least hints at a possibility that the *una sancta* could recognize more than one exclusive form and conception of apostolic succession. Once again, therefore, the cautious form of this text opens up future ecumenical possibilities.

Naturally, the council itself mentioned Protestant ministries only in passing, when it speaks of a *defectus ordinis* in the churches and ecclesial communities born of the Reformation.[73] What does this passage mean? It was observed soon after the council that *defectus* need not mean a total lack but can also mean a simple defect;

more is needed, however, to resolve weighty substantial questions like this than a dictionary and a dash of philological acumen. A theological answer can be inferred only from the total context of the conciliar affirmations, and here it is important to note the clear statement that, while the church of Jesus Christ subsists in the Catholic Church, essential elements of the true church exist outside the Catholic Church.[74] Thanks to these elements, the Spirit of God uses the non-Catholic churches and ecclesial communities as instruments of salvation for their members.[75] Since these bodies are active above all through their ministries, this statement implies a judgment on the ministries of non-Catholic churches and ecclesial communities.[76] The council explicitly states that a valid episcopal and priestly office exists in the Orthodox churches,[77] but its judgment about the ministry in other churches and ecclesial communities is only implicit: on the basis of what has been said, there exist elements of the true ministry in these bodies. Hence both the vocabulary of the council and the logic of the matter show that *defectus ordinis* does not mean a total lack, but a defect in the full form of the ministry.[78]

The council does not define this defect; but in the light of what has been said above, it is surely not only the interruption of the apostolic succession in the episcopal office, since this may not be seen in isolation;

ultimately, this break in continuity was the fruit of a different understanding of the church and of the connection between Gospel and church. The divergence on this point has not yet been overcome. The Second Vatican Council does indeed affirm that the magisterium is not above the Word, but is at the service of the Word; but it does not speak of a polarity between the Gospel and the church in such a way that Scripture would exercise a critical function vis-à-vis the church and the tradition. On the contrary, the council declares that the church does not derive its certainty about revelation only from Scripture,[79] and it emphasizes the inherent unity and interrelation between tradition, Scripture, and magisterium.[80]

This means that it has not been possible for the ecumenical working party to achieve a full consensus on the critical function exercised by Scripture in relation to the church, its teaching, and its praxis. The doctrine that certain ecclesiastical decisions enjoy infallibility makes agreement on this question particularly difficult.[81] When we consider all those points where agreement already exists or may soon be achieved, it becomes clear that the core of the remaining divergence between the separated churches remains the question of the relationship between the Gospel and the church — not the question of the validity of ordinations by nonepiscopal ministers. The question is whether and to what extent the concrete church is the location, sign, and instrument of the Gospel of Jesus Christ.

The Goal: An Agreement to Differ on the Understanding of the Apostolic Succession

Three consequences for the question of a future mutual recognition of ministries can be drawn from these reflections. First, it is not a matter of all or nothing; the mutual recognition of ministries can take place in various stages. Indeed, the concept of a "defect" of the full form of ministry itself entails a certain measure of recognition, and this accords to some extent with the Reformers' own original understanding: for them, ordination outside the apostolic succession was an emergency measure.

Second, this question cannot be resolved in isolation; it must be tackled in the broader context indicated by the words "Spirit," "church," "Word," "sacraments," "ministry."

Third, this means that mutual recognition is a process. At present, the churches have only an imperfect fellowship; the process of mutual recognition of ministries keeps pace with the progress of the churches toward a more perfect and finally a complete fellowship. Recognition of ministries accompanies agreement on questions of ecclesiology and on the relationship between Word and sacrament, both of which build up the church.[82]

A certain asymmetry exists in the relationship of the separated churches during this mutual process of reception, since the various churches and ecclesial communities have different ecclesial forms, each with its own charisms. Accordingly, they make different contributions to the full fellowship that lies ahead of us.[83] Apostolicity in the sense of succession in the episcopal ministry can be communicated only by a church like the Catholic Church, which itself possesses this ministry; the *ecclesia apostolica* subsists in the Catholic Church. This, however, does not reduce ecumenism to a one-way street or a mere "return to the fold." Catholics receive from the churches of the Reformation a richer expression of many substantial apostolic elements, and when Protestants enter the apostolic succession, this succession itself will be enabled to realize its catholicity in a fuller manner.[84] The fullness of apostolicity and catholicity will be completely manifest only at the end of time.

The primary significance of the apostolic succession in the episcopal ministry — the contribution made by the Catholic Church to full ecclesial fellowship — is as an expression of the fact that the church, even in its apostolicity, is never something purely spiritual or intellectual, but is also a tangible historical reality. The Protestant question about the meaning of such a succession in the tradition has the important function of recalling that a mere succession of office-holders is nothing, unless the entire church follows the faith and the spirit of the apostles.[85] Where the Catholic tradition recalls that the specific church and its teaching have a binding character, the Protestant tradition recalls the critical and innovatory function of Scripture, of the living Gospel. It has not yet proved possible to achieve a satisfactory theological and institutional synthesis of these concerns. Such an attempt at reconciliation does not necessarily aim at introducing a completely uniform structure of ministry and succession; here the Second Vatican Council follows Scripture and the patristic tradition in prudently leaving some questions open. The intention rather is to arrive at a common theological evaluation of the institutional structures as such in their relation to the Word and the Spirit, uniting the freedom of the Gospel and of the Spirit who blows where and when he wills (John 3:8) with the fact that God has bound himself and his Spirit to the concrete church.

It is possible that the position of the Orthodox churches can help us find a solution to this problem.[86] These agree in principle with the Catholic Church on the apostolic succession in the episcopal ministry; they too see the concrete church with its episcopal structure as the location, sign, and instrument of the Spirit of God. In one sense, however, they also anticipate (though in a different way) an important concern of the Reformers, since they give the episcopal structure a much more strongly pneumatological basis than does the tradition of the Western church, and they insert this structure more clearly into the totality of the church, understood as communion. This means that the continuity of the apostolic ministry can no longer be understood in terms of a purely historical linear succession; rather, this continuity is realized ever anew in the Holy Spirit and is received and acknowledged afresh by the church.[87] The event of the Spirit founds the institution ever anew. When the freedom of the Spirit is acknowledged in this way within the total sacramental structure of the church, it becomes possible in principle to pronounce a spiritual judgment that acknowledges ministries that are invalid according to purely institutional criteria, but that demonstrate their spiritual worth and fruitfulness.[88]

Unfortunately, this Orthodox position has hardly made any contribution to Catholic-Protestant dialogue until now. It could, however, help make us aware that the great breadth of the patristic tradition, based on

Scripture, to which all the great ecclesial traditions refer, offers a framework for future consensus.[89]

This original breadth and freedom within the church can be regained only by a profounder reflection on the fact that its continuity is guaranteed primarily by the Spirit, and only at a secondary stage by the sacramental signs of institutions. In other words, the institution must be understood as a function of the Spirit, and ecclesiology as a function of pneumatology. As I have shown, the texts of Vatican II offer a number of starting points that must be developed.[90] Once an agreement has been reached within this framework, the form whereby ministers from other churches are to be coopted into the full apostolic succession (understood in the sense of a ministerial succession) poses no major problem.

We may summarize the results of these considerations as follows. If we are to make progress in our understanding of ministry and in the mutual recognition of ministries, the most important precondition is an agreement about the essence of the church, its basic sacramental structure, and its significance for the mediation of salvation. Little attention has been paid to this subject, either in the sixteenth century or in the results of ecumenical discussions about the anathemas of the Reformation period. Only this larger context will allow us to form a judgment about the meaning and scope of the agreements and convergences achieved up to now; for before we can affirm whether the remaining differences and imperfect agreements are of such a nature that they divide the churches, we must first agree about what the church is, and what church unity requires. This is why a discussion of ecclesiology is the most important task on the agenda of future ecumenical dialogue.

– 5 –

Canon Law

*The Normative Application
of Justice and Mercy*

Few pastors today have much good to say about canon law. Prejudices abound: canon law is rigid and inflexible, remote from real life, abstract and incapable of doing justice to the varied, highly diverse situations that make up the concrete reality of human life. This very often leads to an antithesis between legal thinking on the one hand and a pastoral attitude and problem-solving on the other, where law is played off against mercy. For many the two seem to belong to wholly different worlds; indeed, they are diametrically opposed.

If we look at this matter more closely, we see that such prejudices do not result from the law as such, but rather by one particular rigorist application of the law. This merciless, literal justice, with its purely positivistic character, cannot be justified by an appeal to the Bible or to the great canonical tradition of the church, especially as this developed in the high Middle Ages. Reflection on secular theories of law and juridical methodology can help to indicate a way out of the dilemma that many people sense today, enabling us to make a more adequate response to an existential reality that changes rapidly and is subject to individualization.

Mercy as the Fulfillment of Justice

Law is a primal human idea, one of the most fundamental cultural goods. Only law makes a truly human society possible, free from arbitrariness and violence and from a one-sided imposition of the "law of the jungle." Law intends and is able to protect both the freedom of the individual and peace in human society. It is significant that *dikê* is first found among the Greeks, not as a rational, logical concept, but in the mythical form of the goddess who bears this name.

It is arguable that law is the basis of the understanding of God in the Old Testament,[1] whose piety finds a source of absolute trust, of consolation, and of hope in the unshakable conviction that God helps the weak and the poor, establishes justice, and punishes evildoers. This theme is found in many passages in the Psalms and the prophets.[2] This is why in the Old Testament God's covenant with his people has both a theological and a legal dimension. Law and mercy are inseparable here.

The New Testament does not dissolve this connection, but rather reinvigorates it in face of a rigid and merciless understanding of the law in the Judaism of the period. Jesus does not demand a lesser righteousness, but a righteousness greater than that of the Pharisees (Matt. 5:20). In the Old Testament and in Judaism, justice is the essential character of the Messiah and the sign of the messianic age; accordingly, the New Testament bears witness to Jesus as the fulfillment of the Old Testament expectation, the one who proclaims law to the peoples and helps achieve the victory of righteousness (Matt. 12:18, 20). In Jesus' eyes, the kingdom of God and his righteousness belong together (Matt. 6:33). He pronounces a blessing on those who thirst for righteousness or are persecuted for the sake of justice (Matt. 5:6.10), but he reproaches the Pharisees for forgetting justice and love (Luke 11:42).

For Jesus, righteousness — like everything connected with the *basileia* — is ultimately no human achievement, but God's pure gift. This understanding comes to fruition in Paul, who sees righteousness as the gift that God's pure grace makes to us, on the basis of his redemptive act on the cross. In a certain sense, one can say that *dikaiosunê* has the same function in Paul's theology as the concept of *basileia* in Jesus' teaching.

This means that the biblical understanding of righteousness lies close to its understanding of mercy, which is not an emotion of pity, but a reality belonging to salvation history, God's gracious bestowal of mercy on us human beings.[3] Early texts praise Yahweh as gracious and merciful, full of love and faithfulness,[4] and the New Testament makes these affirmations its own.[5] Mercy can be summarized as the event of salvation and redemption in Jesus Christ (Titus 3:6), and God is praised as "rich in mercy" (Eph. 2:4), the "Father of mercy and God of all consolation" (2 Cor. 1:3). Christians must be merciful, as their Father in heaven is merciful (Luke 6:36). As in the Old Testament, God demands that human beings show one another mercy.[6] Mercy is in a special way the characteristic of the Good Samaritan (Luke 10:37). God's love and mercy form one of the main themes in Jesus' proclamation of the kingdom of God.[7]

It follows that we cannot speak of any antithesis in the Old and New Testaments between law (or righteousness) and mercy: both are central to Jesus' message about God's kingdom. Nor can such an antithesis be maintained from the perspective of systematic theology: in Thomas Aquinas's words, *iustitia sine misericordia crudelitas est; misericordia sine iustitia dissolutio* (justice without mercy is cruelty; mercy without justice is weakness).[8] This is because *misericordia* is the fulfillment of *iustitia*.[9] In our conduct toward our neighbor, mercy is the highest virtue, indeed the sum of Christianity.[10]

In keeping with this view, Pope John Paul II writes in *Dives in misericordia:*

> The experience of the past and of our own time demonstrates that justice alone is not enough, that it can even lead to the negation and destruction of itself, if that deeper power, which is love, is not allowed to shape human life in its various dimensions. It has been precisely historical experience that, among other things, has led to the formulation of the saying, *summum ius, summa iniuria* (extreme law, extreme injustice). (12)

Genuine mercy is, so to speak, the deepest source of justice and also its most perfect incarnation, since the equilibrium created by legal justice is limited to the external sphere of material goods, whereas love and mercy bring people to a mutual encounter precisely in that value that human beings' own dignity bestows on them. Love and mercy give persons that which their deepest nature brings them to desire and seek; they accept persons as persons and acknowledge their unique personal dignity. Hence, the fundamental structure of righteousness always enters the sphere of mercy; and mercy in turn has the power to give a new substance to righteousness. It finds its simplest and fullest expression in the act of forgiveness.[11]

We may summarize as follows: mercy does not abolish justice but presupposes it. It leads justice to transcend itself, so that it may find its ultimate fulfillment. Hence, mercy must be the soul of law and justice, which themselves are the necessary presupposition and sine qua non of a civilization of love in which human beings encounter one another as brothers and sisters. Justice without mercy is cold, while mercy without justice would be arbitrary, dishonest, and hollow.

Human Salvation: The Meaning of Canon Law

The church finds its identity in the witness it bears to the kingdom of God in word, sacrament, and action. Its mission is to testify to the kingdom of God and his righteousness and mercy, which have been made manifest in Jesus Christ. In him, the church "is as it were the sacrament, i.e., sign and instrument, of salvation for the human race."[12] The church does not exist for its own sake, but for the sake of the kingdom of God; and this means, in order that human beings may be saved. It is a "sign and instrument" not only as an inner reality, but also as a visible institution, since its visible and invisible, divine and human elements cannot be separated from one another.[13] As a visible human institution, it has a law; traces of this can be discerned even in biblical times. Like the church as a whole, canon law is not an end in itself, but must be understood and practiced as a "sign and instrument" of its salvific task, i.e., as a form of the testimony to righteousness and mercy that the church is called to make.

The church's juridical tradition has expressed the meaning of canon law in the axiom *salus animarum suprema lex* (the highest law is the salvation of souls). This principle has a long history, going back to the great teachers of canon law in the early and high Middle Ages.[14] Thomas Aquinas sees it as the fundamental difference between secular and canon law.[15] Secular law serves to promote peace among human beings, while canon law serves to promote the peace of the church and the salvation of souls. This basic distinction was, however, lost sight of after the period of high scholasticism, until it was rediscovered in the new ecclesiological approaches of the twentieth century. Pope Pius XII repeatedly insisted on this intention of canon law, making it the criterion of the correct application of the law to individual cases, and the Second Vatican Council followed this line; Paul VI likewise recalled it many times. The code of canon law promulgated after the council concludes in a final chord, summarizing and interpreting the whole body of church laws and indicating how they are to be applied: *salus animarum, quae in Ecclesia suprema semper lex esse debet* (the salvation of souls, which should always be the highest law in the church).[16]

In a state under the rule of law, legislation and judicial sentencing must be in harmony with the fundamental constitutive principles that regulate political and judicial life. Analogously, canon law and its application must correspond with the church's ecclesiological self-understanding and with the basic mission entrusted to it, namely, to further the salvation of human persons.[17] If the *salus animarum* defines the goal of canon law, its application in the church must correspond to this principle, which will be the criterion of all ecclesiastical law and legal practice. Only thus will it be obvious that canon law is not an end in itself, but has a function of service: by serving the salvation of human persons, canon law ultimately furthers the coming of the kingdom of God.

Canonical Equity as a Principle for the Application of Canonical Norms

How then can we transpose the goal that gives canon law its definition to the concrete application of laws? More precisely, how can this necessary application take place without emptying positively formulated law of its substance, or even yielding to sheer arbitrariness? What method can preserve us from a rigorous legal positivism that knows no mercy — but also from a false compassion with no firm principles whatever?

The legal tradition of the Eastern churches points here to the principle of *oikonomia*, the legal tradition of the Latin church to the related though distinct principle of *aequitas canonica*, canonical equity, which the concluding canon of the postconciliar code mentions in the same breath as the *salus animarum*. To understand this concept, we must go back to the Greeks.[18] Aristotle discusses *epikeia* in his *Nicomachean Ethics*, where he explains that since general laws can never precisely cover all individual cases, many of which are complex, *epikeia* must fill the gaps.[19] It is the higher justice, which specifies the objective legal norm in individual instances in a flexible and creative manner. It does not disregard the law, but truly belongs to the sphere of justice: *epikeia* is justice for specific cases, ensuring correctness and fairness.

The principle of *aequitas* in Roman jurisprudence is not indeed identical to *epikeia*, but its concern is the same, namely, a humane, moderate, and lenient application of the law appropriate to individual cases. Historians do not agree about whether and to what extent Christian ideas of mercy already made a contribution to the later forms of the Roman doctrine of *aequitas*. This is, however, clearly the case with the canonists of the early and high Middle Ages, who no longer argue exclusively on the basis of the natural law, but do so within the context of salvation history, employing the *aequitas canonica* in their endeavor to unite *iustitia* with the biblical *misericordia*. Outstanding among such canonists were Isidore of Seville, Yves of Chartres, Alger of Liège, Gratian, and Henry of Segusia, who was cardinal bishop of Ostia and is therefore often called Hostiensis. The classical formulation, *aequitas est iustitia dulcore misericordiae temperata,* "equity is justice tempered with the sweetness of mercy," comes from Hostiensis's pen.[20] In concrete individual cases, therefore, *aequitas* is justice mitigated with the help of Christian mercy.

It took the genius of a Thomas Aquinas to bring this conception, which went back to Aristotle and to Roman jurisprudence and had been given depth by the Christian *misericordia,* to a more fully Christian form.[21] Like Aristotle, Thomas is aware that human laws can be valid only *ut in pluribus,* only in the majority of cases. Thanks to their general character, they can never cover all individual instances. *Epikeia* is not above the law; it does not offend against justice, but is the higher justice and the higher virtue, in that it employs an autonomous act of judgment to specify what justice means for the individual case.[22] In his scriptural commentaries, Thomas takes a further decisive step beyond this Aristotelian view. He knows that God accepts each human person in that person's specific and unique situation, and this means that no one is ever simply one case among many in Thomas's eyes: *epikeia* is a personal form of justice, which is led by Christian love to take each human being seriously as a person in a specific situation.[23] "For Thomas, *epikeia* is the *concretissimum* of justice — where justice is understood as personal human justice."[24]

Unfortunately, this idea subsequently fell into oblivion; an important cause of its demise was the restrictive interpretation of *epikeia* and *aequitas* by Francisco Suárez (1548–1617). Only the new ecclesiological reflection prompted by the Second Vatican Council found space for the older and broader traditional concept, which was vigorously maintained by Pope Paul VI in the years after the council. He referred explicitly to the tradition of the high Middle Ages (and especially to Hostiensis) in many of his discourses, describing *aequitas iustitia dulcore misericordiae temperata* as the primary principle guiding the application of the norms of canon law.[25]

The preface to the 1983 Code also states clearly "that canon law is born of the nature of the church" and "that its goal must be in pastoral work, so that people may attain eternal salvation." The following consequence is drawn: "In order to support pastoral work as much as possible, the new canon law is to take account not only of the virtue of justice, but also of the virtues of moderation, humaneness, and cautious prudence, by means of which equity is to be aimed at not only in the application of laws by pastors of souls, but also in the legislation itself."[26] Canon 1752, which brings the code to a close, gives this affirmation the formal force of law.

An Ecclesial Legal Culture Inspired by the Gospel

The fundamental orientation of canon law to the salvation of human beings and the traditional doctrine of *aequitas canonica* are important building blocks for a theory of the application of the norms of canon law, and hence for an ecclesial legal culture inspired by the Bible; in addition a comprehensive reflection on canon law could learn much from secular jurisprudence, which has abandoned the idea that the appropriate legal response can be discerned by means of a logical inference where the norm is the major premise and the facts of the matter form the minor premise. This procedure of logical subsumption does justice neither to the defects inherent in every law nor to the complexity of human lives; a deeper hermeneutical reflection is required.[27] Hence we speak of "jurisprudence" rather than of "juridical science." This is genuinely a *prudence*, which enforces the general norm by matching it to the specific existential situation.[28]

We may formulate the outcome of these reflections as follows: the biblical and the canonical traditions, as well as recent statements by the magisterium, entitle us, indeed require us, to do more than merely apply *aequitas canonica* to those passages where it is mentioned by the present code.[29] Nor is equity only a dynamic principle in the development of law, filling in existing gaps in legislation or legal practice in order to adapt these to changed circumstances. Equity must be acknowledged as the fundamental, comprehensive, and primary principle governing the application of canon law. While *epikeia* is more concerned with the sphere of the personal conscience, *aequitas* belongs in the objective realm of the application of ecclesiastical legal norms. If it is taken into consideration here, it helps prevent canon law from becoming an abstract justice consisting of norms understood literally, something imposed *ab extra* on human persons and their lives, a lethal law that contradicts our human and (*a fortiori*) our Christian sense of what a law ought to be. It aims not at rigidity and formalism, but at flexibility and accommodation. By means of moderation, mildness, and mercy, it aims to realize justice and equity in specific individual cases.

Like love, equity does not abolish justice, but rather applies it concretely and brings it to fulfillment. This means that we must take care not to let equity become arbitrariness, for "if it becomes a 'softening agent in the wash' it is the enemy of law and justice."[30] There is an obvious tension between equity on the one hand and the law's task of ensuring equality and security on the other, and biblical mercy is not the same thing as sentimentality and kindness of heart. It follows that all those who bear pastoral responsibility in the church, especially priests who hear confession and those who exercise judicial or administrative authority, must have a special sense of responsibility and a high legal culture inspired by the Gospel if they are to apply *aequitas canonica* aright. Such a legal culture is not only a question of formal logic. Rather, it is born of the cardinal virtue of prudence and involves a gift of spiritual discernment (*discretio*) in spiritual matters. It demands a wise and understanding heart (1 Kings 3:9, 12) and the ability to discern spirits (1 Cor. 12:10). In the last analysis, all application of law in the church must look to Jesus Christ, the merciful judge.[31] Its criterion must be the *epikeia tou Christou*, the humaneness, kindness, and mildness of Jesus Christ (2 Cor. 10:1).

– 6 –

The Universal Church and the Local Church

A Friendly Rejoinder

The relationship between the universal church and the local church is much discussed today. I myself have written about this,[1] and Cardinal Joseph Ratzinger has criticized my observations in an important and wide-ranging lecture on the ecclesiology of the Second Vatican Council.[2] The questions raised here are so central that they call for further reflection.

An Urgent Pastoral Problem

My remarks were not primarily dictated by a systematic theological interest. Rather, they were born of my pastoral concerns and experience: as the bishop of a large diocese, I have seen the steady widening of the gulf between the norms of the universal church and local praxis.

In many cases, one could go so far as to speak of a mental and practical schism. Many laypersons and priests can no longer understand universal church regulations and simply ignore them. This applies both to ethical issues and to questions of sacramental and ecumenical praxis such as the admission of divorced and remarried persons to communion or the offer of eucharistic hospitality to non-Catholics.

In this situation a bishop cannot be content to be an idle onlooker, but his position is difficult. The episcopal office is the ministry of unity:[3] as a member of the episcopate, the bishop bears responsibility for the universal church in solidarity with the pope and the other bishops, while on the other hand he is the pastor of his local church in solidarity with his clergy and with the questions, expectations, and needs of the faithful who are entrusted to his care. The Second Vatican Council speaks of the bishop's obligation to listen to the faithful and to his clergy.[4]

But how is the bishop to reconcile both these duties today, when the positions diverge so sharply? He is sometimes urged to take "vigorous action," but in many cases this achieves nothing — or precisely the opposite of what he intended. A solution is possible only if the bishop has a certain freedom of action in his application of universal church norms. He must behave responsibly here, not merely trimming his sails to suit prevailing winds. Obviously, no compromise is possible on questions of the faith, and we are entitled to expect that a bishop will bear testimony to the truth "in season and out of season" (2 Tim. 4:2). But in addition to the immutable doctrines of faith and morals, there is a wide sphere of ecclesiastical discipline that does indeed have a more or less close connection with the truths of the faith, but is in principle open to change. In recent decades, the faithful have witnessed many changes that scarcely anyone would have thought possible even fifty years ago.

The church's tradition has developed a number of principles and rules to guide a responsible, flexible application of general regulations to specific situations: the cardinal virtue of prudence, the virtue of *epikeia* (the "higher justice"), canonical fairness, the possibility of dispensation, and indeed the bishop's right to delay action (*remonstratio*). The tradition of the Eastern churches knows the principle of *oikonomia*, the prudent, wise and merciful application of the law in a way that does justice to individual situations.

The employment of such principles is the fruit of the ecclesiological doctrine that a local church is not a province or department of the world church; rather, it is the church in one particular place.[5] The bishop is not a delegate of the pope, but one commissioned by Jesus Christ with a proper responsibility of his own (*potestas propria, ordinaria et immediata*), which is rooted in the sacramental order.[6] He must have all the authority necessary for the governance of his diocese.[7] All this is the unambiguous teaching of the last council.

In the aftermath of the council, however, centralist tendencies have regained their strength. It would be unjust to attribute this only to the curia's greed for power; there is also a justified concern for the situation in some local churches where pluralism and local particularities tend to be exalted in a manner that recalls the ideological traits of an ecclesiastical nationalism, forgetting the New Testament emphasis on unity. The tendency to impose uniformity is also an effect of the globalization that has made the world a "village" in which it is more difficult for the local churches to find solutions of their own, while modern possibilities of communication have made contact with the "central office" much easier. Another contributing factor to the centralizing tendency is the occasional temptation to take the easy way out and abdicate one's own responsibility in favor of "Rome" — the bishop can then hide behind Roman decisions.

Such developments have led to an imbalance in the relationship between the universal church and the local church. This is not some private experience of mine; many bishops on all five continents make the same complaint.[8]

Unfortunately, Cardinal Ratzinger has not chosen to engage in dialogue with these pastoral concerns and experiences. He tackles the problem from a theoretical and systematic perspective and defends a proposition in the 1992 document of the Congregation for the Doctrine of the Faith "On Some Aspects of the Church Understood as Communion," which I and many others have criticized. This Letter affirms that the universal church, "in its essential mystery, is a reality *ontologically and temporally* prior to every *individual* particular Church."[9] He accuses me of holding a view that lacks profound perception of the reality of the church, since it ultimately accepts the existence only of empirical communities.

This is a misunderstanding of my position. One can read the very opposite of such a view in the essay he criticizes, as well as in many earlier publications.[10] The sociological reduction of the church to individual communities is precisely the position against which I have fought in my years as bishop, and I have often been attacked for taking such a stance.

This problem is so important, both pastorally and (as we shall see) ecumenically, that I should like to set out my views once again, this time more on the level of fundamental theological principles.

Historical Perspectives

One cannot clarify the relationship between the universal church and the local church by means of abstractions and deductions alone. The church is a historical reality; it is the church's history, under the guidance of the Spirit of God, that provides the exegesis of what it is. Every answer to our question must therefore do justice to the concrete history of the church, which of course is highly complex. We must be content here with only brief indications.

If we turn first to Scripture, we find that "the local community is the focal point of interest" for Paul.[11] The primary referent of *ekklêsia* in his main epistles is the individual church or community, and this allows him to speak of local *ekklêsiai* in the plural. For Paul, each local community is the manifestation of the one church of God; thus, he speaks of "the church of God which is in Corinth" (1 Cor. 1:2; 2 Cor. 1:1; see also Rom. 16:1). The church of God is present in each local church. In the captivity epistles, usually considered deutero-Pauline, this local use of *ekklêsia* is virtually absent; in both Ephesians and Colossians, "each use of this term envisages the universal church as a whole, not the local community."[12] In Luke's writings, *ekklêsia* can mean both the house church and the local community. We also find a "holistic ecclesiological conception" in Luke.[13]

The reflection of the early church begins with the local churches led by a bishop, where the one church of God is present.[14] This presence gives birth to a *communio* between the individual churches,[15] which finds expression above all in the requirement that at least three bishops take part in the ordination of a new bishop[16] and in the synods attended by neighboring bishops from as early as the third century. A number of canons at Nicaea (325) incorporate the individual local churches with their bishops into provinces, and these provinces into districts which later came to be called patriarchates.[17] A similar structure was drawn up at the synod of Sardica (c. 343),[18] which established a procedure that took account of what we would call the principle of subsidiarity. This shows that the specific importance of the local church did not make it autonomous; each had its own place in a network of *communio* consisting of metropolitan provinces, patriarchates, and ultimately the universal church.

Within this network of *communio*, Rome claimed from an early date to possess a responsibility and authority vis-à-vis the universal church; Ignatius of Antioch attributes a "presidency in love" to the church of Rome.[19] This does not yet amount to the attribution of a primacy in teaching and jurisdiction, but it does mean that "the Roman church is the leading and decisive authority in that which constitutes the essence of Christianity."[20] Rome had an undisputed authority as the leading episcopal see, as we see clearly in canon 3 of the Council of Constantinople (381) and canon 28 of the Council of Chalcedon (451). This gave the bishop of Rome a decisive moral authority and a prestige that, while not constituting jurisdiction over the Eastern churches, was much more than a mere primacy of honor. The ecclesiology of the first millennium thus succeeded in avoiding a one-sided emphasis on either the local church or the universal church.

This historical fact — which we have only sketched briefly here — has a fundamental theological significance, since the church of the first millennium, whose patrimony is common to all the churches, has a decisive importance. It was Joseph Ratzinger himself who put forward the thesis in a lecture held at Graz in 1976 that "what was possible for a whole millennium cannot be impossible for Christians today.... Let me make the point in other words: Rome need not require that the East accept a higher doctrine of the primacy today than that which was formulated and lived in the first millennium."[21] This "Ratzinger formula" won wide acceptance and has become a fundamental principle in ecumenical dialogue.

It is significant because of the universalistic conception of the church that developed in the West in the second millennium, after the schism between East and West. Ultimately, this ecclesiology derived all authority in the church from the authority of the pope.[22]

This view was accepted by Bonaventure,[23] but it remained foreign to so great a theologian as Thomas Aquinas.[24] Nevertheless, it prevailed in the struggles against conciliarism, the Reformation, modern state absolutism, Gallicanism, and Josephinism. This development seemed to have found its definitive seal with the teaching of the First Vatican Council (1869–70) on the jurisdictional primacy of the pope and with the 1917 code of canon law.

The Second Vatican Council attempted through its teaching on the local church, on the sacramentality of episcopal ordination, and on episcopal collegiality to repristinate the patristic conception and harmonize it with the teaching of the First Vatican Council. The *communio*-ecclesiology that was elaborated in the period after the council sought to develop the indications given in the conciliar texts, and the Extraordinary Synod of Bishops in 1985 took up this discussion and affirmed *communio* as the central and fundamental idea of the Second Vatican Council.[25] This has also proved extremely fruitful in ecumenical discussions, where *communio* has become a central concept in the description of ecumenical goals.[26]

The Letter of the Congregation for the Doctrine of the Faith *Communionis Notio*, "On Some Aspects of the Church Understood as Communion," takes a basically positive attitude to this discussion, but rightly criticizes an ecclesiology that takes a one-sided starting point in the local church and leads to an understanding of the universal church as a logically posterior coalition of local churches. The local church and the universal church pervade each other. The Congregation expands the conciliar statement that the universal church consists "in and out of" the local churches by affirming the thesis that the local churches exist only "in and out of" the universal church. Finally, the Letter argues, against some theologians who affirm the primacy of the local church, that the universal church has historical and ontological priority.

In view of the historical evidence, this last thesis is problematic and was much criticized. This was obviously the reason for the official clarification published a year after the Letter had first appeared.[27]

Common Ecclesiological Presuppositions

Before I discuss this thesis, I should like to ward off potential misunderstandings as far as possible by stating the points where I am in complete agreement with Cardinal Ratzinger's position. The shared conviction, which every genuinely Catholic theology must accept, can be summarized as follows.

First, Jesus Christ wanted only one single church, and this is why our creed professes faith in the *una sancta catholica et apostolica ecclesia.* Just as we profess faith in the one God and the one redeemer Jesus Christ and the one Spirit and the one baptism, so it is with the one church. We do not regard this oneness as something lying only in the future, the result of our ecumenical endeavors; it does not only exist at present in the fragments of separated churches, but "subsists" in the Roman Catholic Church. In other words, despite all the weakness of the Roman Catholic Church, God's faithfulness preserves the one church in it: this is the concrete location of the one church.[28]

Second, the one church of Jesus Christ exists "in and out of" local churches,[29] since the one church of Jesus Christ is present in every local church, especially in every celebration of the Eucharist. Since, however, the one Lord Jesus Christ is present in every local church, none can exist in isolation: it can survive only in fellowship with all the other local churches. Just as the universal church exists "in and out of" local churches, so too every individual church exists "in and out of" the one church of Jesus Christ. The church's unity is a *communio*-unity, which excludes egotism and national autonomy on the part of any local church. The local church includes the universal church, and the universal church includes the local church.

Third, just as the local churches are not branches or provinces of the universal church, so the universal church is not the sum or product of a combination of local churches. The local church and the universal church inhere in each other; their relationship is one of compenetration or circumincession. The church is neither a federal nor a unitary state; it has a constitution of its own that cannot be adequately grasped by any sociological analysis. Ultimately, its unity is a mystery, since its archetype is the Trinity of the one God in three Persons.[30] This is why unity does not mean uniformity; the unity of the church does not exclude plurality, but rather includes it.

I believe that these three theses show my basic agreement with *Communionis Notio*. Henri de Lubac coined a pregnant formulation for the essential point here: "Since there is a mutual indwelling and inclusion, there is also a perfect correlation."[31] However, the Congregation's Letter goes beyond this thesis of a mutual indwelling and correlation when it speaks of a primacy of the universal church. Such a thesis depends for its plausibility on the arguments that can be made in its favor; it is valid only to the extent that these arguments hold water.

Controversy about a Scholastic Dispute

In his response, Cardinal Ratzinger explains and defends the thesis of the historical and ontological primacy of the universal church over the local church both from a historical and a systematic perspective.

He finds support for his affirmation of the historical primacy of the universal church in the account of the Pentecost event in the Acts of the Apostles: "The Church is manifested, *temporally,* on the day of Pentecost in the community of the one hundred and twenty gathered around Mary and the twelve Apostles, the representatives of the one unique Church and the founders-to-be of the local Churches, who have a mission directed to the world: from the first the Church *speaks all languages.*"[32] However, this argument cannot go unchallenged.

Many exegetes believe that the account in Acts is a Lukan construction; it is probable that Christian communities existed in Galilee, too, from the beginning. Michael Theobald has pointed out that Luke's interest in his Pentecost narrative is not the universal church but the Jewish diaspora that is gathered together for the feast and that widens in the course of time, under the guidance of the Holy Spirit, to become the church formed out of all the peoples. According to Theobald, normative character belongs to this process — not only to Luke's story of how the church began on the first Pentecost feast.[33] Clearly, Cardinal Ratzinger himself is aware of the weakness of his historical argument, since he admits that a purely historical demonstration is difficult; however, the ultimate point is not historical evidence, but the inner relationship between the universal church and the local church. This is why the question of the ontological primacy is more important.

What does this mean? Cardinal Ratzinger now makes a surprising move, when he justifies the ontological primacy of the universal church by means of the thesis of the preexistence of the church. This thesis was developed by the church fathers, who appealed to Paul's words about "the Jerusalem above" as "our mother" (Gal. 4:26) and to the image of "the city of the living God, the heavenly Jerusalem, the community [*ekklêsia*] of the firstborn who are enrolled in heaven" (Heb. 12:22f.).[34] Such thinking reflects the idea, widespread in contemporary Judaism, that the Torah already existed in the heavenly sphere before creation; parallels can be found in other religions and in Platonism.[35]

If one detaches the thesis of preexistence from the time-conditioned forms in which it is expressed, we may say that it affirms that the church is not the outcome of chance constellations, developments, and decisions within history: it has its foundation in God's eternal will to bring salvation and in his eternal salvific mystery. It is precisely this that Paul's Letters proclaim when they speak of God's eternal mystery of salvation, which was hidden from earlier ages but is now revealed in and through the church (Eph. 1:3–14; 3:3–12; Col. 1:26f.).

No one would dispute the preexistence of the church if the concept is understood in this way; this is one of the essential theological presuppositions of every ecclesiology. One may, however, ask what specific support this concept offers to the ontological primacy of the universal church. Who is to say that preexistence can be predicated only of the universal church and not of the concrete church that exists "in and out of" local churches? Why may not the one church preexist as a church "in and out of" local churches? Accordingly, the thesis of the preexistence of the church provides no evidence in favor of the thesis of the primacy of the universal church. It can equally provide evidence in favor of the simultaneity of the universal church and the local churches, the thesis that I myself and many others propose.

Many historical and substantial arguments suggest that we should understand the preexistence of the church in terms of the concrete church "in and out of local churches." No less a theologian than Henri de Lubac affirms: "A universal church that exists antecedently to all the individual churches, or that is conceived as existing in itself independently of the local churches, is merely an abstraction."[36] This is because God loves not bloodless abstractions but concrete human beings of flesh and blood. God's eternal salvific will intends the incarnation of the Logos and envisages the concrete church in the flesh of the world.

On closer inspection, the controversy about the primacy of the universal church can be seen for what it is — not a question of ecclesial doctrine, but of theological opinion and of the various philosophies employed by the theologians, which either find their starting point with Plato in the primacy of the idea and the universal, or else follow Aristotle in seeing the universal as realized in the concrete.[37] Naturally, the latter intellectual tendency does not mean a reduction to empirical phenomena alone. The medieval controversy between those theologians who thought more in Platonic terms and others who thought more in Aristotelian-Thomistic terms was a dispute between schools within the common faith of the church. Both Bonaventure and Thomas Aquinas, who took different paths on this question as well as on the question of the universal authority of the pope, are recognized as doctors of the church and venerated as saints. Why should a plurality that was possible in the Middle Ages no longer be possible today?

The Ecumenical Perspective

Our reflections on the relationship between the universal church and the local church have considerable consequences for the pastoral problems that I mentioned at the beginning of this essay. I saw this originally as a pastoral problem within the Catholic Church, but it has now also become an urgent ecumenical concern for me, since our goal is not a church of uniform unity, but a church that can agree to differ — in Joseph Ratzinger's words, the churches must remain churches, while becoming ever more *one* church.[38] Hence, the ecumenical process aims at the *communio*-unity of the churches, or better, the *communio*-unity of the church.[39]

Our ecumenical dialogue-partners will find our proposal of this goal credible only if we ourselves realize the relationship between universal and local church — as unity in plurality and plurality in unity — in an exemplary manner in our own church. A one-sidedly universalistic perspective will awaken painful memories and provoke mistrust: it will frighten off other Christians. This means that it is important for dialogue with the Orthodox and Protestant churches and ecclesial communities to demonstrate that a local church (and in exactly the same way, a patriarchate, a united Protestant church, and every other confessional grouping) can be the church of Jesus Christ in the full sense only in fellowship with the universal church. We must also demonstrate that such a *communio*-unity does not crush or absorb the local churches and their legitimate traditions, but rather accords them a space of legitimate freedom: for only so can the whole fullness of Catholicism be realized in concrete terms.[40]

A balanced relationship between the universal church and the local church does not contradict the Petrine ministry in the church: on the contrary, it corresponds to the inner meaning of this ministry, which has the task of "strengthening the brethren" (Luke 22:32), i.e., strengthening the bishops and their local churches and keeping them united with one another.[41] Pope John Paul II has issued the invitation to a fraternal ecumenical dialogue about how this can be done in the future.[42] If the pope himself offers such an invitation, it cannot be improper to express one's honest opinion about the correct definition of the relationship between the universal church and the local church.

– 7 –

Ecumenical Perspectives on the Future

One Lord, One Faith, One Baptism

When we reflect under the biblical title "One Lord, one faith, one baptism" on ecumenical perspectives for the future, we must bear in mind that we can have a future and indeed shape a future for ourselves only if we know where we are coming from. Otherwise, we will confine ourselves to pseudo-prophetical gesturing and construct utopias based on nothing more substantial than wishful thinking.

The Changed Situation

The Second Vatican Council declares that one sign of the working of the Holy Spirit in our times is the new reaction of all the churches to their division: namely, repentance and a yearning and positive search for unity. After centuries of separations, ghetto-building, hostility, or mutual indifference, all the churches have set out on the ecumenical path.

It is significant that the ecumenical movement should have begun at the World Missionary Conference at Lausanne in 1927: at that time, the participants realized that the division among Christians was one of the greatest obstacles to world mission. In Germany, the trenches of the Second World War and the concentration camps of the Third Reich were birthplaces of ecumenism. Christian confessors, Catholic and Protestant, were imprisoned together with Jews. Their shared opposition to an inhuman and criminal regime revealed the depths of what they had in common — and showed that this was greater than what divided them.

After the Second World War, ecumenical theology was able to build on these experiences. Prominent Catholic and Protestant theologians discovered the riches of each other's church. They read Scripture together and studied the church fathers together. This exchange of views deepened and enriched their own faith, showing them that they were much closer than they had thought. Max Metzger, a Protestant pastor who bore witness with his blood to the cause of peace between the peoples and the religious confessions, is an important name in this context; we should also mention Karl Barth, Karl Rahner, Yves Congar, Hans Urs von Balthasar, Hans Asmussen,

Peter Brunner, Edmund Schlink, Heinrich Fries, and many others.

The theological movement was supported and accompanied at the "grass roots." Movements of population in the aftermath of the war meant that there were now few purely Catholic or Protestant regions in Germany: Catholics and Protestants were neighbors and worked together. They learned to appreciate each other as human beings and as Christians. The "typical" Catholic or Protestant environment no longer existed.

It is certainly true that this led to a problematic diminution in people's awareness of their Catholic or Protestant faith. It is, however, impossible to reverse these sociological developments; all we can do is to look forward, uncovering and strengthening what people believe in common and searching for unity in faith. There is no alternative to ecumenism! The question is not *whether* we wish to draw closer together; the only issue is *how* to do this in a correct and responsible manner. The ecumenical movement itself is an irreversible process, both in spiritual and in existential terms.

The Ecumenical Breakthrough

Naturally, such a process is accompanied by difficulties and resistance. It takes more than a single day to fill in trenches that have divided people for centuries;

nor can one simply hop over them, since no church can allow itself to deny the tradition and the faith of its fathers and mothers. Faith involves deep convictions of the human conscience that cannot lightly be exchanged in the way that one changes a shirt or buys a new automobile.

This explains why the ecumenical movement initially encountered a position of extreme reserve on the part of the church's magisterium; it was more or less condemned by Pius XI in his encyclical *Mortalium Animos* (1928), which declared that since the Catholic Church is the true church of Jesus Christ, non-Catholic Christians must return to the unity of the Catholic Church. Fear that ecumenism would lead to a relativization and watering down of the Catholic position prompted the Vatican to prohibit Catholic theologians from taking part in ecumenical events. This prohibition was slightly relaxed under Pius XII in an Instruction by the Holy Office (1949), but the pope maintained the thesis in his encyclical *Mystici Corporis* (1943) that the Catholic Church *is* the church of Jesus Christ and the body of Christ, and such a one-to-one identification leaves de facto no place for ecumenism with other churches.

However, not all official statements by the magisterium are intended to enjoy perennial validity. Ecumenical awareness and the longing for unity won acceptance in the Catholic Church too. As long ago as the closing years of the nineteenth century, there had been the Mechlin conversations in Belgium with Anglicans. Abbé Couturier founded "spiritual ecumenism" in France, leading to the so-called *nouvelle théologie*. Yves Congar — initially the object of criticism and suspicion, later created a cardinal after the council — was the theological pioneer of ecumenism. The "Jäger-Stählin group," founded in 1945, played an important role in Germany. Lorenz Jäger, archbishop of Paderborn and later a cardinal, founded the Johann Adam Möhler Institute in Paderborn in 1957. In Holland, Jan Willebrands (another who subsequently became a cardinal) and Frans Thijssen founded the "Catholic conference for ecumenical questions" in 1952. In the course of his journeys through Europe, Willebrands met Augustin Bea in Rome. Bea — later a cardinal — was the first president of the Secretariat for Unity, which Pope John XXIII set up in 1960; Willebrands became his deputy and succeeded him in this office in 1969.

The Second Vatican Council (1962–65) brought the official breakthrough. As nuncio in Bulgaria and Turkey, Pope John XXIII had come to know and appreciate the Orthodox Christians and their churches. He wanted the council to have an ecumenical dimension; this is why he founded the Secretariat for Unity and invited non-Catholic observers, who were given the opportunity to make their comments on the documents in preparation.

Ecumenism left its mark on the fundamental constitution on the church, *Lumen Gentium*, which made one important alteration with regard to *Mystici Corporis*. Where Pius XII had affirmed that the Catholic Church *is* the church of Jesus Christ, the council affirmed more cautiously that the church of Jesus Christ "subsists" (*subsistit*), i.e., finds its concrete realization and presence, in the Catholic Church. This made it possible to say that not only individual Christians, but as elements of the church of Jesus Christ itself, exist de facto outside the visible structure of the Catholic Church — and not merely as sad relics of the past, but elements with an inner dynamism that impels toward full unity.

On this basis, *Unitatis Redintegratio*, the conciliar decree on ecumenism, elaborated "Catholic ecumenical principles" and drew practical consequences. This decree begins as follows: "The restoration of unity among all Christians is one of the principal concerns of the Second Vatican Council," and this made ecumenism one of the priorities of the postconciliar church. In his encyclical on ecumenism, *Ut unum sint* (1995), Pope John Paul II explicitly affirms his commitment to this cause. He has often repeated that the ecumenical option taken by the council is an irrevocable decision.

Naturally, the council maintains that the Catholic Church is the true church, the church that has remained faithful to the apostolic inheritance. But it also teaches that ecclesial reality (not "the church" as such) exists outside the Catholic Church. These ecclesial elements are above all the proclamation of the Word of God and the baptism by which one becomes a member of the church. Faith, hope, and love, signs and testimonies of holiness, and indeed martyrdom are all found outside the Catholic Church. The Orthodox churches also possess the Eucharist and the episcopal ministry in the apostolic succession. The council goes so far as to state that the Holy Spirit makes use of these churches and ecclesial communities as instruments whereby their members can be saved.

The basic conciliar position is taken up by the postconciliar canon law codes of the Latin church and the Eastern Catholic churches: this makes ecumenism a juridical obligation, especially for the bishops. As far as I know, no other church has a canon law that imposes this particular obligation! The Ecumenical Directory (first versions 1967 and 1970; revised version 1993) specifies the practical application of the council's statements and makes them binding on bishops and priests. The directory does in fact give the local churches a much larger freedom than is often supposed. Finally, we must mention the prophetical encyclical *Ut unum sint*, in which Pope John Paul II makes a positive assessment of the results of ecumenical dialogue up to that point and declares ecumenism one of the priorities of his pontificate.

I know of no other church leader who has spoken so frequently and clearly in favor of ecumenism as John Paul II.

At this point, someone might object: "What about *Dominus Iesus?*" Has not this document, issued by the Congregation for the Doctrine of the Faith in August 2000, reversed everything and put an end to all ecumenical hopes? Many people think so, many have been disappointed and hurt by this declaration — and this has hurt me too, since the sadness and pain of my friends makes me sad and pained. I must, however, add my impression that many of those who exaggerate the importance of this document are persons who never took ecumenism seriously. Now they are delighted to find confirmation of their own view that ecumenism is a waste of time.

I do not wish to play down *Dominus Iesus*, but I would like to try to indicate the proper framework for understanding it. The document does not intend to offer a comprehensive presentation of Catholic doctrine on ecumenism. All it wishes to do is to recall a number of conciliar statements that are in fact well known. Unfortunately, it does this in a manner that I find unnecessarily sharp and harsh. This is why *Dominus Iesus* must be read in the context of other, more comprehensive — and also more authoritative — texts such as the conciliar statements and the encyclical *Ut unum sint*. It has no power to invalidate those texts, nor to cancel the many positive ecumenical statements and actions by the pope in the period since August 2000 that show that "Vatican policies" have not changed. We have not gone back to the era before the council! Rather, as the pope says in *Novo millennio ineunte* (2001), the council remains the compass on the church's path into the new century and the new millennium.

Where Are We Now?

A great many positive things have happened on all levels in the decades since the council, and we cannot turn the clock back (even if wished to do so). Close collaboration and friendships have grown up in parishes and associations of Christians, and shared liturgies of the Word and encounters are a feature of every Christian community; the same is true on the levels of theological faculties, dioceses, and episcopal conferences. Instead of mutual opposition or ignorance there is a new cooperation and openness, so that Christians work together wherever this is possible. There exists a genuine — though as yet imperfect — fellowship among the churches.

Progress on the level of the universal church was made visible by a number of ecumenical events during the Holy Year. For the first time in history, the holy door in St. Paul's Outside-the-Walls was opened jointly by the pope, the archbishop of Canterbury, and a delegate of the Ecumenical Patriarch of Constantinople in the presence of representatives of twenty-three churches and church fellowships — more than during the council itself. They went on to celebrate an impressive act of worship together. The same happened in front of the Colosseum in Rome when the martyrs of the twentieth century were commemorated. Both times, the positive transformation of the ecumenical situation was obvious.

At present, the Council for Unity is conducting official dialogues with thirteen churches or world federations of churches and has more informal contacts with others. This involves more than the Catholic-Protestant relationship, which is so important in Germany: we have dialogues with the ancient Oriental churches (Armenians, Copts, Syrians, Ethiopians, Malankara Church, and the Assyrian Church of the East), the Byzantine Orthodox churches (especially the Ecumenical Patriarchate of Constantinople, the Russian Orthodox Church, the Greek, Serbian and Romanian Orthodox churches, etc.), the Anglican Communion, Lutheran and Reformed churches, Methodists, Baptists, Mennonites, Adventists, the Disciples of Christ, new evangelical and Pentecostal communities, and others — a broad spectrum that does not leave us time to fall into a boring routine! The Roman Catholic Church is not a member of the World Council of Churches but has good relations with this body: a "Joint Working Group" meets annually to discuss important topics. The Roman Catholic Church is a formal member of the "Faith and Order" Commission, which we consider the most important WCC institution.

Ecumenical work is not limited to these official theological dialogues. Just as important — perhaps even more important — are the many personal encounters and visits. The pope is in frequent epistolary contact with other church leaders. Visits from patriarchs and other church leaders to Rome are frequent events, and the pope too makes ecumenical contacts in the course of his apostolic journeys. Such visits and letters are more than mere formal diplomatic courtesies. This kind of contact allows the churches to resume forms of *communio* (i.e., of ecclesial fellowship) that were common in the first millennium.

This fellowship is not only the fruit of some human sense of sympathy and solidarity; it is more than a humanistic philanthropism. It is based on our shared faith in Jesus Christ and on our common baptism, thanks to which all the baptized are already members of the one body of Christ. Sadly, this already existing fellowship is not yet a full and complete union, as we see in the fact that it is not yet possible for us to gather together around the table of the Lord and celebrate the Eucharist, the sacrament of unity. It goes without saying that we must yearn for this and do all we can to bring the day of fulfillment nearer.

Two Milestones along the Ecumenical Path

I should like to mention two milestones along the path to full unity, where our dialogues have led to official results. First, there are the agreements with the ancient Oriental churches, which separated from communion in the fourth and fifth centuries in connection with the councils of Ephesus (431) and Chalcedon (451) and the profession of faith that Jesus Christ is truly God and truly a human being in one Person. Thanks to thorough preliminary theological work, promoted above all by the "Pro Oriente" Foundation, which Cardinal Franz König founded in Vienna, the pope and the various patriarchs have been able to issue joint declarations affirming that the differences on the level of formulations and the underlying philosophies do not affect the substance of the faith itself. Even if our formulations differ, we are professing in substance the same faith.

Second, on October 31, 1999, the Common Declaration on the Doctrine of Justification was signed in Augsburg. This was the central point of conflict in the Reformation period, defined by Martin Luther as "the article on which the church either stands or falls."

Luther's own personal experience is central to this conviction. He was deeply troubled by the question: "Where can I find a gracious God?" How can I stand my ground before God, how can I be just? Luther realized that his own works could not justify him: this was possible only if he accepted in faith that God declared and made him just, not because of his own works, but in view of the cross of Christ, in whom alone is salvation. This is indeed the heart of the Gospel: the question of salvation and of interior peace.

In other words, we were not divided by some peripheral issue, but by the central question of the Gospel. It took years of preliminary study on the national and international levels before we were able to say that we agree on basic doctrines of justification and that the mutual condemnations of the past are no longer aimed at today's partners in dialogue. This was not the outcome of some ecclesiastical diplomatic trade-off, nor was it a weak compromise; it was never intended that one church should yield to the other and abandon its own patrimony, for no church can do that. Rather, we have learned to understand each other's teaching at a new and deeper level in the light of Scripture and of the patristic tradition that we share; this has also meant examining afresh Luther's writings and the decrees of the Council of Trent. Finally, we were able to affirm honestly that we have so much in common that the remaining differences no longer divide our churches. We discovered the existence of a unity in plurality, or (to use another common phrase) a difference that presented no obstacle to reconciliation.

The signing of this declaration in Augsburg had — rightly — the character of a celebration and was marked by thanksgiving services throughout the world, even in regions such as Latin America where there are very few Lutherans. It was in fact only in Germany that negative reactions were registered. This showed that many persons were unaware of the international theological discussion that had made Augsburg possible and now felt surprised and even tricked.

The pope immediately greeted the signing in Augsburg, and this ought to dispose of any lingering doubts. The highest authorities in the Catholic Church explicitly support the declaration, and in fact the Holy See has frequently declared its approval.

The pope called Augsburg a "milestone." This is a precise definition of what was achieved. We have covered an important stretch of the road, but we have not yet attained our goal. Nevertheless, we have achieved much: we agree in professing our faith in the heart of the Gospel, and the one baptism makes us all members of the one body of Christ. This allows us to bear common witness to the good news of the Gospel in a world that knows less and less about the Gospel, yet needs it more than ever. The ecumenical Kirchentag, the German church conference in 2003, was given the task of testifying to our common faith, to what unites us and gives our life meaning. We must tell the world what we can do together, and we must not let this great opportunity go to waste — as we would do, if we were to concentrate one-sidedly on the question of what we cannot yet do together.

The Ecclesiological Question That Remains Open

When we ask what full unity would mean, we at once see which questions still remain open. What is the goal of the ecumenical pilgrimage, and what are the next steps? The Catholic answer is clear: unity in faith, in the sacraments, and in ecclesial ministries. According to Catholic and Orthodox understanding — and according to the position that the Old Catholic churches too held until the 1970s — a celebration of the Eucharist in common is not possible until we have attained a substantial consensus on these issues. According to 1 Corinthians 10:16–17, there is a unity between sharing in the one eucharistic body of Christ and sharing in the one ecclesial body of Christ. According to the tradition that was shared and considered valid until the 1970s, eucharistic and ecclesial fellowship belong together.

This fact, however, suffices to make it clear that the one church cannot be a uniform church: unity must not be confused with uniformity. On the one hand, it is not possible for contradictory positions on questions of the faith to be tolerated alongside one another; it is not acceptable for one church to formulate binding expressions of its faith while another church rejects these and anathematizes them as offenses against the Gospel. On the other hand, however, it is perfectly possible for the one faith to find a variety of expressions in different accents, rites, traditions, and customs. This plurality is not a defect! On the contrary, it means richness and fullness. It is catholicity in the true sense of that word.

This is what "unity in plurality" and "plurality in unity" mean. Patient dialogue can help us understand the antithetical positions that divide us today as different approaches to the one mystery, not mutually exclusive but rather complementary. Contradictory affirmations can become complementary affirmations: the differences then present no obstacles to reconciliation.

We have not yet reached this point; our differences await reconciliation. But it is not only dogmatic teachings that are unreconciled. Our unreconciled hearts present an even greater problem. All the churches have their collective memories of what "the others" did in the past, memories that generate grave suspicions about "the" Catholics, "the" Protestants, or "the" Orthodox. We need a "purification of the memory" based on a fresh reading of history. Pope John Paul II showed the way forward here on the first Sunday in Lent 2000, when he asked pardon for the sins committed against Christian unity.

Only this spirit of forgiveness and reconciliation can help us deal with the remaining dogmatic differences. The consensus we have reached on the substance of the Gospel, on Jesus Christ and justification, makes the question of the church and its ministries all the more urgent, since the church is witness, sign, and instrument of the Gospel message. This is why the theological dialogues and the consultation process set in motion by the Faith and Order Commission of the WCC are presently studying the topic "Nature and Purpose of the Church."

Catholics and Orthodox have the same understanding of the church. We share the creeds of the early church, the same sacraments (especially the Eucharist), and the same episcopal church constitution. This reduces the ecclesiological problem to the question of the Petrine ministry. The Orthodox, too, acknowledge Rome as the first apostolic see with a "primacy in love" (to use the phrase of St. Ignatius of Antioch), but they hold the two dogmas of the First Vatican Council (1869–70) about the pope's universal jurisdiction and infallibility to be incompatible with their own understanding of *koinônia*/communio.

Unfortunately, discussion of this topic has become much more difficult since the political revolutions in central and eastern Europe in 1989–90. With the return of freedom to the former communist states, it was possible for the uniate churches in the Ukraine and Romania, which Stalin had brutally suppressed in 1946, to resume their visible, public existence. This meant that the Orthodox church lost many of its parishes, and these two Eastern Catholic churches have been repeatedly accused by Moscow and other Orthodox churches of "uniatism" and proselytism. The last plenary assembly of the Joint International Theological Commission at Baltimore in 2000 did not make any headway on these questions. It is clear that many prejudices still need clearing up; but many contacts since then have made me more confident that we may soon be able to take a step forward here.

A Different Understanding of the Church

In the case of the churches and ecclesial communities born of the Reformation in the sixteenth century, the ecclesiological gulf is wider, since it is not only the Petrine ministry, but the understanding of ministry in general that is problematic. What is the relationship between the priesthood of all believers and the special priestly ministry, and what of the episcopal ministry in the apostolic succession? There is as yet no consensus about what the church is and what its constitutive ministries and sacraments are; discussion is made more arduous by the fact that the churches of the Reformation give various answers to these questions. A synodal resolution of the French Reformed Church even goes so far as to call in question the significance of baptism as a foundational element of the church.

Dominus Iesus brought these ecclesiological questions out into the open. Many of our Protestant friends were offended by the passage in this document that says that the communities born of the Reformation in the sixteenth century are not "churches" in the true sense of the word.

This point could certainly have been made in a friendlier manner, in terms less open to misunderstanding. But *Dominus Iesus* does not in fact deny that these bodies are "churches." It says only that they are not churches in the sense in which the Catholic Church understands itself to be a "church," and this is surely undeniable! In terms of their own ecclesiology, they have no desire whatever to be a church like the Catholic Church. They are a different type of "church." They do not possess the episcopal ministry in the historic succession, nor the Petrine ministry; but for us Catholics, both these elements are essential.

Nevertheless, they are not simply "non-churches." They possess essential ecclesial elements, especially the proclamation of God's Word and baptism. As the encyclical *Ut unum sint* says, there is not simply an ecclesial vacuum outside the Catholic Church. Although "the church" does not exist there, there is an ecclesial reality with a dynamic inherent propulsion toward full ecclesial life. This is why the episcopal ministry is a central theme in today's international ecumenical discussion.

A declaration of the Protestant church in Germany, *Church Fellowship in Protestant Understanding* (September 2001), notes "that Protestants must oppose the Catholic position on the necessity and form of the 'Petrine ministry' and the primacy of the pope, the understanding of apostolic succession, the refusal to admit women to the ordained ministry, and not least the role of canon law in the Roman Catholic Church." This formulation is so harsh, so devoid of nuances and uninterested in the outcome of ecumenical dialogues up to this point, that it makes *Dominus Iesus* appear a positive ecumenical text by comparison. At any rate, these words make it clear that we still have a great deal of work to do if we are to clarify all the doctrinal questions in the ecumenical sphere!

These divergent positions have consequences for the question of eucharistic fellowship. It is easy to grasp why so many people long for this (and not only in the context of events like the Kirchentag in 2003). Division at the table of the Lord is particularly painful. Accordingly, I cannot understand how the declaration *Church Fellowship* can formulate the antitheses between the churches so harshly, without any attempt at compromise — and in the same breath issue an invitation to the most intimate form of church fellowship. How are these compatible?

Catholic canon law does envisage individual circumstances — not general situations — where grave necessity makes possible pastoral solutions in view of the good of souls. It is my impression that these regulations are interpreted generously. Nevertheless, they cannot be applied to the situation of a Kirchentag, where many other kinds of ecumenical services can be held (agape celebrations, Vespers, Taizé prayer, vigils, etc.), using words and symbolic gestures to express the ecumenical fellowship that has already been attained — but without giving the false impression that we already have full unity.

Certainly, we cannot be content with this state of things: the ecumenical process must go further, and in fact the international dialogue on these questions is making progress, as we see in the Porvoo Statement of the Scandinavian Lutheran churches and the Anglican Communion, in the Agreement between the Lutheran churches in the United States and Canada and the Episcopalian Church, in the document of the Catholic-Anglican dialogue, *The Gift of Authority*, and in documents of the multilateral dialogue, especially the Lima Declarations. These show that the churches are drawing closer on questions of ecclesiology and church ministry, especially in their understanding of the episcopal office, and this entitles us to be hopeful: consensus may not yet exist, but it is clear that the ecumenical movement is not stagnating.

In his encyclical *Ut unum sint*, Pope John Paul II himself has issued an invitation to a patient fraternal dialogue about the future exercise of the Petrine ministry. This is a courageous — indeed, a revolutionary — step for a pope to take, and it has given vigorous impetus to a broad theological debate. The Vatican Council for Unity has studied all these responses carefully.

Naturally, the pope did not call the Petrine ministry as such into question. That would have been impossible, since Catholics believe that this ministry is a gift of God to his church. In a world that has largely become a "global village," yet remains marked by tremendous inner tensions and conflicts, the Petrine ministry of unity is certainly not obsolete. Indeed, the tensions among Orthodox and Protestants show how healthy it is to possess the kind of common point of reference and ministry of unity that we have in the papacy.

The mode of exercise of this ministry has undergone wide-ranging changes in the course of history, and it will continue to change in coming generations too. The unity that the Petrine ministry safeguards need not mean the uniform ecclesiastical administration that has developed de facto in the Latin church. How then is this ministry to exercise its service of unity in the future in such a way that it does not infringe upon the relative autonomy of the other traditions, especially those of the East? How are we to achieve a new unity in plurality? How can we establish the correct equilibrium between the universal and the local ecclesial dimensions?

We are only at the beginning of this discussion within the Catholic Church, but to judge from many contributions to the last consistory of cardinals in May 2001 and the synod of bishops in October of the same year, we have every reason to be optimistic.

A Turning Point Has Been Reached

The ecumenical movement cannot be reversed. But it is also true to say that it has reached a turning point: while we must continue the difficult task of studying our ancient controversies and trying to resolve them, this alone is not enough — as the signing of the Common

Declaration on the Doctrine of Justification showed. Most Christians were happy that the old controversies had found a resolution, but in fact very few really understood the matter at issue. The questions of the sixteenth century had ceased to interest them.

Luther had asked how he, as a sinner, could be certain of his salvation, and he found the liberating answer in the apostle Paul's Letter to the Romans: thanks exclusively to faith in the righteousness that is God's gift on the basis of the cross of Christ. Our experience today, however, is no longer the crushing burden of sin, but the absence of any experience of sin. This in turn has its roots in the experience of the absence of God and in people's indifference to God. Most people today have no idea what is meant by "sin," still less by original sin, redemption through the cross, or the mediation of salvation through the sacraments of the church. Our question is not: "How do I find a gracious God?" We ask: "Is there any connection between my life and God at all?" For very many people, God is tremendously remote — perhaps still the ultimate horizon of their lives, but no longer the center. We have all become more or less Deists, no longer asking: "How can I do what God expects?" but "How can I do justice to myself and to my own life?" The ancient answers offered by all the churches (Catholic, Protestant, Orthodox) are no longer comprehensible and have ceased to interest people.

This confronts all the churches with a new common task, a new ecumenical challenge. They must display anew the riches of their own specific traditions and learn how to proclaim who God is for us and who we are before God, who Jesus Christ is and what he means for us. We must learn anew how to say what sin, judgment, and grace mean. We must translate our traditions into a language that affects and illuminates our lives and is capable of kindling hope. At the beginning of a new century and a new millennium, the churches face the ecumenical challenge of a new evangelization.

In such a situation, people do not want to squander their time on theological hairsplitting and church-political games. They want answers from the Gospel that will help them to live their daily lives. They sense more and more that the secularized answers are a sham that cannot give them the support they seek. Such answers can only disappoint. More persons than we usually suppose are asking questions — consciously or unconsciously — about God, grace, and salvation. They have high expectations of us, and we must not disappoint them! Today and in the future, however, answers can be found only in a common enterprise. Ecumenism is not an optional luxury tacked onto the rest of the church's task. On the contrary, ecumenism is central to this task, a pastoral priority for all the churches. We must work together in a new evangelization to ensure that the new century will be more peaceful than the last — for that is people's deepest yearning.

Courage for the Ecumenical Task

I should like to conclude by looking to the ecumenical future. I am convinced that there is no alternative to ecumenism. Jesus' explicit charge to his disciples compels us to pursue this task. Division is sin, because it is such an obvious contradiction of Jesus' will. Accordingly, we must not allow present difficulties to frighten us into withdrawing from dialogue. Ecumenism is the work of the Spirit of God, and who would try to stop the Spirit? This means that we must be people of hope!

Hope is not at all the same thing as wishful thinking or merely academic utopias. For the Bible, hope is linked to *hupomenê*, usually translated as "patience." Literally, it means: holding out under a heavy burden. Charles Péguy called patience "hope's younger sister."

The Spirit of God does not meekly follow the timetables that we draw up: God's time is not the same as human time. We must be content with doing what is possible and necessary today, looking to the great goal of visible unity and confident that it will be attained.

We must be realistic. This means first that we do not underestimate the difficult questions that remain open, and second that we take proper account of the intensified search by all the churches in recent years for their own identity — a process that also generates resistance to ecumenism. This resistance is not confined to the Catholic Church; in the Orthodox churches, the concept of "ecumenism" has frequently taken on negative associations, and ecumenical reservations on the part of Protestants were expressed unambiguously when the Common Declaration was signed in Augsburg. The decision by the Council of Protestant Churches in Germany to stop using the Catholic translation of Scripture in ecumenical acts of worship is a conscious retreat from a consensus that had been achieved only after great effort.

I can understand why many people who feel that the ecumenical process is too slow say that "official" ecumenism is running in place, or even going backward. Is there then a "crisis of ecumenism"?

It is undeniable that the ecumenical enthusiasm that was so tangible immediately after the Second Vatican Council no longer exists; many factors have contributed to this changed situation. But must this be interpreted as a sign of crisis? Would it not be better to speak of a process of maturation? After the youthful enthusiasm of the first years, we have now entered a process of growth where we see that reality is not as uncomplicated as we once thought. We have, however, achieved much, and now, in this situation of transition, we must engage in a responsible dialogue in love and truth.

In the coming years, this dialogue in love and truth will be less of an academic debate and more a *dialogue of life*, since our separation is not the fruit of theological discussion, but rather of a process of mutual alienation that means that we no longer understand one another. We must learn to live with one another again, collaborating in every way that is possible today without any infringement of ecclesiastical regulations — and more important, without acting against our own consciences. And this means doing a great deal more in common than we are doing at present!

Sadly, it is still necessary to break down misunderstandings and prejudices. The "purification of memory" remains an important task, and we have still much to learn about one another. This entails not discussion, but communication, the exchange of each other's gifts. We can learn much from one another, but only if we are willing to acknowledge our own deficits: there is no ecumenical dialogue without personal conversion and institutional renewal, and we begin not by "converting" our dialogue partner, but with our own conversion and renewal. Instead of demanding that our partners take steps in our direction that their conscience does not yet allow them to take, we should be the first to reflect on how we might move in their direction — and our steps may give them the courage to set out toward us.

Dialogue in love is accompanied by dialogue in truth, for love without truth is empty, dishonest, and ultimately deceitful. Ecumenical progress does not mean that we abandon the convictions of our own faith, but rather (as with the doctrine of justification) that we penetrate these more deeply, until we reach the point at which they are compatible with the convictions of the faith of the other church. This requires serious theological work; laity, clergy, and bishops must all be trained in the ecumenical spirit, not least because the fruits of the preparatory work achieved in our various dialogues remain largely unknown. They must be "received" by the church as a whole.

Accepting this intermediary stage and living it in positive terms does not mean giving up the ecumenical goal of visible church unity. More fellowship has been achieved in the past forty years than in the four and a half centuries since the Reformation, and this encourages us to look to the future with hope, rather than to abandon the path. Ultimately, we ourselves cannot create unity. The unity of the churches is a gift of the Spirit of God: this is why prayer for unity is the heart of the ecumenical process.

Notes

Chapter 1: The Diaconate

1. F. Lepargneur, "Ein Diakonat für Lateinamerika," in *Diaconia in Christo*, Quaestiones Disputatae 15/16, ed. K. Rahner and H. Vorgrimler (Freiburg: Herder, 1962), 469ff.
2. Ibid., 431.
3. Ibid., 482ff.
4. *Lumen Gentium* 29.
5. *Lumen Gentium* 28f.; see also 41; *Orientalium Ecclesiarum* 17; *Ad Gentes* 16.
6. *Lumen Gentium* 21.
7. H. Vorgrimler, *Sakramententheologie* (Düsseldorf: Patmos, 1987), 288.
8. *Philadelphians* 4; *Smyrnaeans* 12:1; *Ephesians* 2:1; *Magnesians* 2:1.
9. *Apostolic Tradition* 8.
10. *Didascalia Apostolorum* 2:44.
11. *Ephesians* 2:1.
12. *Apostolic Tradition* 8; see also *Didascalia* 2:44.
13. Polycarp, *Philippians* 5:2, quoted in *Lumen Gentium* 29.
14. W. Kasper, "Dank für 25 Jahre Ständiges Diakonat," *Diaconia Christi* (Rottenburg a.N., 1994), 24.
15. *Trallians* 3:3, quoted in *Lumen Gentium* 41.
16. *Ad Gentes* 16.

17. *Sacrosanctum Concilium* 35:4; *Dei Verbum* 25.
18. *Ad Gentes* 16; see also 7 canons 1008f.
19. H. Hoping, "Diakonie als Aufgabe des kirchlichen Leitungsamtes," *Dokumentation 13 der AG Ständiger Diakonat in der Bundesrepublik Deutschland* (Beyharting, 1996), 34.
20. *Lumen Gentium* 9.
21. Ibid., 1, etc.
22. W. Kasper, *Die Communio-Ekklesiologie als Grundlage für eine erneuerte Pastoral* (Rottenburg a.N., 1990), 5.
23. *Commentary on John* 26.6.13, quoted in *Sacrosanctum Concilium* 47, etc.
24. Kasper, *Die Communio-Ekklesiologie als Grundlage für eine erneuerte Pastoral*, 19.
25. See *Lumen Gentium* 10.
26. Ibid., 16.
27. Ibid., 16f.
28. See *Gaudium et Spes* 1.
29. H. Pompey, "Not der Menschen unserer Zeit — als Wegzeichen Gottes für den Ständigen Diakonat," *Dokumentation 11 der AG Ständiger Diakonat in der Bundesrepublik Deutschland* (Beyharting, 1994), 20ff.
30. R. Zerfaß, "Der Beitrag des Caritasverbandes zur Diakonie der Gemeinde," *Caritas* (1987), fasc. 1.
31. D. Schad, "Selbstverständnis der Diakonie und diakonisches Profil sozialer Arbeit," *Diakonie* (1996), fasc. 6, 354.
32. R. Zerfaß, *Lebensnerv Caritas* (Freiburg: Herder, 1992), 66.
33. [Translator's note: Many deacons in Germany work fulltime on the same economic basis as priests, namely, as paid ("stipendiary") ministers. The others ("nonstipendiary") have

full-time jobs and exercise their ministry mostly in the evening or on weekends.]

Chapter 2: Priestly Office

1. See 1 Cor. 9:1; 15:8; Gal. 1:1, 13.
2. See *In Ioannem*, 6.7.
3. Rom. 16:25–27; Eph. 3:9–11; Col. 1:25–27.
4. Rom. 12; 1 Cor. 12.
5. *Lumen Gentium* 21.
6. *Lumen Gentium* 28; *Presbyterorum Ordinis* 2; *Christus Dominus* 30.
7. *Sacrosanctum Concilium* 42.
8. *Lumen Gentium* 28.
9. IV *Sent.* 13.1.
10. *Lumen Gentium* 10.
11. *Ep.* 66.8.
12. *Sermo* 340.1, quoted in *Lumen Gentium* 32.
13. *Summa Theologiae* (*STh*) III 82.7 ad 3; Suppl. 31.1 ad 1; *Summa contra Gentiles* (CG) IV 73.
14. *Ep.* 14.4.
15. *Lumen Gentium* 37; *Presbyterorum Ordinis* 9.
16. See 1 Peter 5:3 ("being examples to the flock") in the Latin translation: *forma facti gregis ex animo* (literally: "having yourselves become wholeheartedly the form which the flock is to take").
17. [Translator's note: Cardinal Kasper refers here to the practice in the German and Austrian churches, where laypersons with the same theological training as priests work full-time in ministry as salaried "pastoral assistants."]

18. Rom. 16:1–16; Phil. 2:25; 4:3; Col. 4:10–15; Philemon 1, 24.

19. *Lumen Gentium* 33; *Apostolicam Actuositatem* 24.

Chapter 3: Episcopal Office

1. See H. W. Beyer, *kubernêsis*, *Theologische Wörterbuch zum Neuen Testament* (*TWNT*) 3:1034–36; in English see *Theological Dictionary of the New Testament*.

2. STh II-II, 184,8 ad 1. In another passage, Thomas uses equally dramatic language when he calls the bishops *duces exercitus Christiani*, "generals of the Christian army" (*Summa contra Gentiles* (CG) IV, 60).

3. A. von Harnack, *Dogmengeschichte*, 3:468ff. H. Küng, *Das Christentum: Wesen und Geschichte* (Munich: Piper, 1994), 493ff., presents a similar position. See pp. 96–113 below.

4. L. Ott, *Handbuch der Dogmengeschichte*, IV/5, 24, 43, 46–48, 50, 80–87; Y. Congar, *Handbuch der Dogmengeschichte*, III/3c, 109.

5. *Lumen Gentium* 21.

6. See Die deutsche Thomas-Ausgabe, 24:341ff.; O. Pesch, *Thomas von Aquin: Grenze und Größe mittelalterlicher Theologie: Eine Einführung* (Mainz: Matthias-Grünewald, 1988), 57ff., 66ff., 70, 376.

7. Congar, *Handbuch der Dogmengeschichte*, III/3c, 127–38.

8. M. D. Chenu, *Das Werk des hl. Thomas von Aquin*, Die deutsche Thomas-Ausgabe, suppl. vol. 2), 2d ed. (Graz: Styria, 1982), 39ff. In English see Chenu, *Toward Understanding Saint Thomas* (Chicago: Regnery, 1964).

9. Pesch, *Thomas von Aquin*, 373ff.

10. Congar, *Handbuch der Dogmengeschichte*, III/3c, 175–82.

11. On this problem, see M. Seckler, *Das Heil in der Geschichte: Geschichtstheologisches Denken bei Thomas von Aquin* (Munich: Kösel, 1964), 217ff.

12. M. Grabmann, *Die Lehre des hl. Thomas von der Kirche als Gotteswerk: Ihre Stellung im thomistischen System und in der Geschichte der mittelalterlichen Theologie* (Regensburg, 1903); Congar, *Handbuch der Dogmengeschichte*, III/3c, 150–56; G. Sabra, *Thomas Aquinas' Vision of the Church: Fundamentals of an Ecumenical Ecclesiology* (Mainz, 1987).

13. STh I, 1,7: *Omnia autem pertractantur in sacra doctrina sub ratione Dei.*

14. See Seckler, *Das Heil in der Geschichte*, 33ff.; Chenu, *Das Werk des hl. Thomas von Aquin*, 343ff.

15. STh I-II, 106,4 ad 4. This affirmation is central to Thomas's debate with Joachim of Fiore, whose view he calls *stultissimum* ("utterly stupid"). On this, see Seckler, *Das Heil in der Geschichte*, 189–95. On the differences between the responses made by Thomas and Bonaventure to Joachim, see J. Ratzinger, *Die Geschichtstheologie des heiligen Bonaventura* (Munich: Schnell & Steiner,, 1959), 117–20.

16. STh III, 8,1 ad 3. See Grabmann, *Die Lehre des hl. Thomas von der Kirche als Gotteswerk*, 184–93; Sabra, *Thomas Aquinas' Vision of the Church*, 94–104.

17. STh II-II, 183,2 ad 2. See Congar, *Handbuch der Dogmengeschichte*, III/3c, 152 n. 97.

18. STh I-II, 106,1. Other passages are cited by Congar, *Handbuch der Dogmengeschichte*, III/3c, 155 n. 119.

19. These words recall in particular Augustine's *De Spiritu et Littera*.

20. See Congar, *Handbuch der Dogmengeschichte*, III/3c, 153.

21. STh I-II, 65,5.

22. See Seckler, *Das Heil in der Geschichte*, 240–51.

23. Sent. IV, 17,3,1 sol. 5; 27,3,3 ad 2; STh III, 64,2 ad 3.

24. In Exp. Super ad Rom. 1,1 a similar significance is attached to the proclamation of the Gospel and to the sacraments: *evangelium autem idem est quod bona annuntiatio, annuntiatur enim in ipso coniunctio hominis ad Deum, quae est bonum hominis.* At In Rom. 1,6 Thomas says that the Gospel not only announces salvation, but also confers salvation in faith: *per evangelium homo consequitur gratiam sanctificantem.* The *materia evangelii* is Christ himself (In Rom. 1,2), who dwells in our heart by faith (1,6). Rep. Super ad Timotheum I 4,2 attributes a similar significance to the Word of God and to the Eucharist: *verbum enim Dei est spirituale nutrimentum quo sustentatur anima, sicut corpus per cibum.*

25. See pp. 96–113 below.

26. STh I-II, 106,1.

27. STh III, 60,2.

28. STh III, 63,6; 73,2, etc. On this, see pp. 96–113 below.

29. STh III, 65,5.

30. Suppl 37,2; CG IV, 75. See Grabmann, *Die Lehre des hl. Thomas von der Kirche als Gotteswerk*, 267–94.

31. IV Sent 24,3,2; Suppl 40, 4–5 among the *Annexa sacramento ordinis*.

32. Rep. Super ad Timotheum I 1,2: *Ad praelatum pertinet primo quod doceat de forma fidei, ne fides subditorum corrumpatur.*

33. Rep. Super ad Timotheum II 4,1.

34. STh III, 67,2 ad 1, with reference to Acts 6:2 and 1 Cor. 1:17.

35. STh III, 67,1 ad 1. On the distinction between the teaching ministry of the bishop (*cathedra pastoralis*) and that of the master of theology (*cathedra magistralis*) (IV Sent. 19,2,2 qua.

3 sol. 2 ad 4; Ql III, 4,1), see M. Seckler, "Kirchliches Amt und theologische Wissenschaft," in *Die schiefen Wände des Lehrhauses* (Freiburg: Herder, 1988), 105–35; 111–15.

36. STh II-II, 184,1 ad 2; ibid., 2 and 3; Opusculum De perfectione vitae spiritualis, 1 (PVS).
37. STh II-II, 184,5.
38. STh II-II, 184,6; 185,1 ad 2; see Suppl 35,1; 36,1.
39. STh II-II, 185,4: *Et ideo nihil prohibet aliquos esse perfectos qui non sint in statu perfectionis: et alios esse in statu perfectionis qui non sint perfecti.*
40. STh II-II, 184,7. On Ps.-Dionysius and his influence on medieval ecclesiology, see Congar, *Handbuch der Dogmengeschichte,* III/3c, 145–49.
41. STh II-II, 185,1.
42. STh II-II 184,5; 185,4f., etc. This is an important argument for Thomas: it leads him to reject the participation by priests and bishops in warfare, which was customary during his period, as an *abusus*. Priests and bishops should shed their own blood for others rather than shed others' blood. Thomas makes a clear distinction here between the secular and the spiritual *potestas* (STh II-II, 40,2).
43. STh II-II, 185,1.
44. STh II-II, 184,6 ad 1; 185,1 ad 1; Ql I, 7,2 (14).
45. STh II-II, 185,1 ad 1.
46. STh II-II, 184,7 ad 2; 185,4.
47. STh II-II, 185,2.
48. STh II-II, 183,1.
49. STh II-II, 184,4 and 5; PVS 24.
50. STh II-II, 184,7.
51. PVS 15.

52. STh II-II, 184,5 ad 3; 185,1 ad 1.
53. STh II-II, 184,7.
54. STh II-II, 184,2 ad 3; PVS 14.
55. STh I-II, 108,1.
56. STh II-II, 183,4.
57. STh II-II, 184,1.
58. STh I-II, 65,5.
59. STh II-II, 183,4 ad 1; 184,1.
60. Car 3.
61. Car 11 ad 6. O. H. Pesch is probably right to suggest that this statement reflects the spirituality of the Order of Preachers, to which Thomas himself belonged, and hence is an expression of his own position (*Thomas von Aquin*, 66f.).
62. STh II-II, 184,6; PVS 20ff.; Ql I, 7,2; III, 6,3. These affirmations must be read against the background of the bitter debates between the mendicant orders and the secular clergy in the thirteenth century: see Die deutsche Thomas-Ausgabe, 24:343ff., 419f.
63. See the overview in Die deutsche Thomas-Ausgabe, 24:369ff., and the detailed study by U. Horst, "Darf man das Bischofsamt erstreben? Thomas von Aquin und die Sonderstellung des Bischofs in der Kirche," in *Für euch Bischof — mit euch Christ*, Festschrift for Cardinal F. Wetter, ed. Manfred Weitlauff and Peter Neuner (St. Ottilien: EOS, 1998), 179–93. On what follows, see STh II-II, 185,1.
64. Horst, "Darf man das Bischofsamt erstreben?" 193.
65. STh II-II, 185,2.
66. STh II-II, 184,7 ad 1. See n. 164 below.
67. STh II-II 184,7 ad 3; see 182,1 ad 1.
68. STh II-II, 185,4.

69. STh II-II, 185,5.
70. On this, see Congar, *Handbuch der Dogmengeschichte*, III/3c, 127–35.
71. STh II-II, 185,6 and ad 1.
72. STh II-II, 185,1 ad 1.
73. STh II-II, 185,7.
74. STh II-II, 184,7 ad 1.
75. STh II-II, 185,7 ad 4.
76. Suppl 40,3.
77. CG IV, 56.
78. STh III, 61,1.
79. It appears to be Thomas's merit to have introduced the idea of the instrumental causality of the humanity of Christ into the doctrine of Christ as Head of the church: Congar, *Handbuch der Dogmengeschichte*, III/3c, 152 n. 100. J. R. Geiselmann, "Christus und die Kirche nach Thomas von Aquin," *Theologische Quartalschrift* 107 (1926): 198–202; 108 (1927): 233–55, demonstrates the doctrinal development in Thomas's thinking on this point.
80. CG IV, 56.
81. Ibid.; STh III, 62,1 and 5.
82. STh III, 8,5.
83. CG IV, 74.
84. STh III, 65,3 ad 1: *Sed bonum commune spirituale totius Ecclesiae continetur substantialiter in ipso Eucharistiae sacramento.* Suppl 37,2; 37,4. See Congar, *Handbuch der Dogmengeschichte*, III/3c, 153 n. 104; see also n. 28 above.
85. STh II-II, 37,4; III, 63,6; 65,3; 73,3; Suppl 37,2. 4; 38,1; CG IV, 74f.
86. STh III, 65,3 and ad 2.

87. STh III, 82,1; CG IV, 74f.; Suppl 37,2; 37,4 ad 1; 40,4.
88. STh III, 61,4.
89. Suppl 36,2.
90. See n. 4 above. A bibliography on Thomas's position is found in Ott, *Handbuch der Dogmengeschichte*, IV/5, 81 n. 3. For a nuanced review of the development in Thomas's thinking on this question, see J. Lécuyer, "Les étapes de l'enseignement thomiste sur l'épiscopat," *Revue Thomiste* 57 (1957): 29–52.
91. IV Sent. 24,3,2 and Suppl 37,3 include the priest, the deacon, and the subdeacon in the *ordo*, but not the bishop. Suppl 37,1 ad 2 attributes to the priest the *plenitudo huius sacramenti*, while the bishop has the *plenitudo auctoritatis* (Suppl 37,2) or the *completa potestas* (ibid., 38,1 ad 5).
92. Ps.-Dionysius, *Ecclesiastical Hierarchies* 5,1,5–6.
93. Lécuyer speaks of a "certaine impression de gêne" and an "impression de manquer d'une parfaite unité" ("Les étapes de l'enseignement thomiste sur l'épiscopat," 34, 51).
94. IV Sent. 7,3,1 sol. 2 ad 3. Thomas consistently maintains this position thereafter (see n. 97 below).
95. IV Sent. 94,3,3 sol. 2.
96. IV Sent. 13,1,1 sol. 2 ad 2; see 23,1,3 sol. 2 ad 3; CG IV, 76; STh III, 82,10 ad 2.
97. IV Sent. 24,3,3; STh III 82,1 ad 4; Suppl 36,2 ad 1; 38,2 ad 2; 40,5.
98. IV Sent. 24,3,2; Suppl 40,4 ad 3: the *repraesentatio Christi* by the bishop takes place *in hoc quod alios ministros instituit et Ecclesiam fundavit*.
99. CG IV, 76.
100. STh III, 82,1 ad 4; Suppl 37,2; 38,1.
101. Suppl 36,2.

102. Rep. super ad Philippenses 1,1; Rep. super ad Titum 1,2; PVS 21. 23; STh II-II, 184,6 ad 1.

103. Rep. super ad Timotheum 1,4,3; Rep. super ad Timotheum 2,1,3; Rep. super ad Hebraeos 6,1; STh II-II, 184,5.

104. Lécuyer summarizes these witnesses as follows: Augustine, the Venerable Bede, the Glossa Ordinaria, Isidore of Seville, the Decretum of Gratian, Innocent I, the Council of Laodicea, etc. ("Les étapes de l'enseignement thomiste sur l'épiscopat," 45).

105. According to Epiphanius, he was a radical fourth-century critic of the imperial church and of its hierarchical structures: see H. C. Brennecke, "Aërios," *Lexikon für Theologie und Kirche*, 3d ed. 1:185f.

106. Rep. super ad Titum 1,2; Art. Fid. 425; STh II-II, 184,6 ad 1.

107. See Lécuyer, "Les étapes de l'enseignement thomiste sur l'épiscopat," 40–45.

108. PVS 24; Suppl 40,5; Quodl III, 6,3 ad 5: *episcopatus est ordo in comparatione ad corpus mysticum*.

109. PVS 21.

110. STh III, 72,1 ad 3; 73,6.

111. See Ignatius of Antioch, Letter to the Smyrnaeans 8,1.

112. The inconsistency — and the problem that Peter Lombard continues to pose for Thomas — lies in the question of whether episcopal ordination confers a *character sacramentalis*. This is denied at IV Sent 24,3,3,2, although episcopal ordination is said to confer a *potestas spiritualis*, and this is what is intended by a "sacramental character"; see also Suppl 39,1 ad 2 and 40,5. Thomas justifies his position by arguing that the episcopal office is not immediately ordered to the Eucharist and that it

consequently lacks the *deputatio ad cultum* that is essential for the sacramental character (STh III, 63,1).

113. See Congar, *Handbuch der Dogmengeschichte*, III/3c, 104–6, 140.

114. Bonaventure does not agree with Thomas in inferring a differentiated understanding of *ordo* from the distinction and the connection between *corpus Christi verum* and *corpus Christi mysticum*. For Bonaventure, the episcopate merely adds a *dignitas* and an *officium* to priestly ordination, but not a new degree of the *ordo* (IV Sent. 24,2,2,3). In other words, Bonaventure does not diverge at all from Peter Lombard. He reinterprets the other witnesses in the church's tradition (who were important for Thomas) in keeping with Lombard (ibid., ad 1–3).

115. See H. de Lubac, *Corpus Mysticum: l'eucharistie et l'église au Moyen Âge, Étude historique*, 2d ed. (Paris: Aubier, 1949); A. Volk, *Theologie der Eucharistie* (Munich: Kösel, 1973).

116. Following Augustine, the connection between the Eucharist and the church is frequently set out in the documents of the Second Vatican Council. See *Sacrosanctum Concilium* 36; *Lumen Gentium* 3, 7, 11, 26. In precisely the same way, Thomas speaks of the Eucharist as the sacrament of unity and of love (STh III, 73,3 ad 3; 82,2 ad 3). Naturally, the Council takes a decisive step beyond Thomas by acknowledging episcopal ordination as the fullness of the sacrament of orders (*Lumen Gentium* 21), breaking with medieval tradition by ceasing to understand episcopal ordination on the basis of priestly ordination. Now it is priestly ordination that must be understood on the basis of episcopal ordination.

117. See J. Ratzinger, "Der Einfluß des Bettelordensstreites auf die Entwicklung der Primatslehre," in idem, *Das neue Volk*

Gottes: Entwürfe zur Ekklesiologie (Düsseldorf: Patmos, 1969), 51–71. On the following paragraph, see Congar, *Handbuch der Dogmengeschichte*, III/3c, 154f.; Sabra, *Thomas Aquinas' Vision of the Church*, 125–32.

118. IV Sent 24,3,3; Contra errores Graecorum II, 32–36; CG IV, 76; Suppl 40,6.

119. See Congar, *Handbuch der Dogmengeschichte*, III/3c, 118f., 125f. Ultimately, this doctrine goes back to Leo the Great (ibid., 13f.).

120. STh II-II, 88,12 ad 3; III, 72,11 ad 1. Other passages are cited in Congar, *Handbuch der Dogmengeschichte*, III/3c, 154 n. 114; Sabra, *Thomas Aquinas' Vision of the Church*, 131 n. 41.

121. STh II-II, 39,1.

122. STh II-II, 89,9 ad 3.

123. IV Sent 7,3,1 ad 1.

124. Contra errores Graecorum II, 32.

125. STh II-II, 1,10; see 11,2 ad 3; Contra errores Graecorum II, 36; CG IV, 25; De potentia 10,4 ad 13. We cannot discuss here the important question of how this position affected the development of an explicit doctrine of papal infallibility; this happened only after Thomas's death.

126. As is argued by Congar, *Handbuch der Dogmengeschichte*, III/3c, 144.

127. Bonaventure, *Breviloquium* 6,12: *fons, origo et regula cunctorum principatuum ecclesiasticorum, a quo tamquam a summo derivatur ordinata potestas usque ad infima Ecclesiae membra.*

128. II Sent 44 exp. text.: *a papa gradus dignitatum in Ecclesia et disponuntur et ordinantur.*

129. IV Sent 18,1,1,2 ad 2: *Omnis potestas spiritualis datur cum aliqua consecratione.*

130. IV Sent 24,3,2,3 ad 3. Whereas there is a generic difference between the *potestas* of the priest and that of the bishop, there is no such difference between the *potestas* of the bishop and that of the pope (Suppl 40,6 ad 3). Naturally, Thomas has no doctrine of the collegiality of the episcopal office.

131. This is clearly stated in many passages in the polemic text *Contra impugnantes*. See Sabra, *Thomas Aquinas' Vision of the Church*, 131f.

132. Suppl 34,1 ad 1.

133. Suppl 34,2 ad 3.

134. STh II-II, 185,2 ad 2.

135. STh III, 8,6.

136. STh III, 65; see 82,6; Suppl 34,4 ad 2. This is why Ql V, 7 calls him a *persona publica*.

137. STh II-II, 183,2 ad 2 f.

138. Suppl 34,2; 35,2. On the essence of the sacramental character as *signum configurativum* with Jesus Christ and as the handing on of authority, see STh III, 63,3.

139. STh III, 8,6; 78,1; 82,1; 82,6; 82,7 ad 1.

140. STh III, 62,5.

141. STh III, 8,6.

142. STh III, 62,1; 64,1.

143. STh III, 8,5 ad 1: *per solam personalem actionem ipsius Christi*. Suppl 36,3 ad 2: the *ministri* are *quodammodo instrumenta illius effluxus qui fit a capite in membris*.

144. Suppl 34,5 sets out the *ex extrinseco* of the sacraments in general.

145. Suppl 34,1 ad 3; 36,3.

146. Ver 14,10 ad 11.

147. STh II-II, 43,5.

148. STh I-II, 107,4.
149. Ver 17,5.
150. Ver 17,4 obi.4 and ad 4. On this, see Pesch, *Thomas von Aquin*, 378ff., who points out the ecumenical relevance of this position.
151. STh III, 8,3. On this, see M. Seckler, "Das Haupt aller Menschen," in *Die schiefen Wände des Lehrhauses*, 26–39. It is in this context that the traditional thesis of the *ecclesia ab Abel* has its place: see Y. Congar, "Ecclesia ab Abel," in *Abhandlungen über Theologie und Kirche*, ed. Reding (Düsseldorf, 1952), 79–108.
152. STh II-II, 183,2. 3; 184,4; Suppl 34,1; 37,1, etc. See Grabmann, *Die Lehre des hl. Thomas von der Kirche als Gotteswerk*, 305–7.
153. On this, see J. Ratzinger, *Volk und Haus Gottes in Augustins Lehre von der Kirche* (Munich, 1951; reprint 1992), 281–85; Y. Congar, *Handbuch der Dogmengeschichte*, III/3c, 6–8.
154. On this, see Seckler, *Das Heil in der Geschichte*, 220ff.
155. STh I-II, 106,4; III, 53,24. See n. 15 above.
156. CG IV, 76.
157. CG IV, 83: *in praesenti ecclesia, quae regnum Dei dicitur.*
158. STh III, 60,3.
159. STh III, 73,4.
160. CG IV, 76.
161. STh II-II, 183,2 ad 3.
162. STh I-II, 3,4 ad 1: earthly peace is related to the *beatitudo* of heaven *antecedenter et consequenter.*
163. IV Sent 24,3,2; Suppl 40,4 ad 3; 7. On the church as *sponsa Christi* in Thomas, see Grabmann, *Die Lehre des hl. Thomas von der Kirche als Gotteswerk*, 251–58.

164. In the specific context of his discussion of property or poverty (STh II-II, 184,7 ad 1), Thomas speaks of serenity (*aequanimitas*) as the attitude proper to a bishop. However, in the light of the fundamental eschatological attitudes of *hypomonê* and *parrhêsia* in the New Testament and of the meaning of "serenity" in the spiritual tradition of the mystics (see R. Körner, "Gelassenheit," *Lexikon für Theologie und Kirche*, 3d ed. 4:403–4), this affirmation takes on the character of a basic principle.

Chapter 4: The Apostolic Succession

1. J. Ratzinger, *Theologische Prinzipienlehre: Bausteine zur Fundamentaltheologie* (Munich: E. Wewel, 1982), 251; Eng. trans: *Principles of Catholic Theology: Building Stones for a Fundamental Theology*, trans. Mary Frances McCarthy (San Francisco: Ignatius Press, 1987). A similar verdict is given by O. Karrer, one of the earliest ecumenists: "The decisive controversial issue between the Christian confessions is...apostolicity": "Apostolische Nachfolge und Primat," in *Fragen der Theologie heute*, ed. J. Feiner, J. Trutsch, and F. Bockle (Einsiedeln: Benziger, 1957), 176; see also idem, "Apostolizität der Kirche," *Lexikon für Theologie und Kirche*, 2d ed., 1:765. These two articles by Karrer give a good overview of ecumenical discussion before the Second Vatican Council. Additional studies are listed in *Reform und Anerkennung kirchlicher Ämter: Ein Memorandum der Arbeitsgemeinschaft ökumenischer Universitätsinstitute* (Munich and Mainz, 1973), 157–62, and in F. Mildenberger, "Apostel/Apostolat/Apostolizität IV," *Theologische Realenzyklopädie* 3:477. The following are particularly important: R. Groscurth, ed., *Katholizität und Apostolizität: Theologische Studien einer gemeinsamen Arbeitsgruppe zwischen der römisch-katholischen Kirche und dem Ökumenischen Rat der Kirchen*, supplementary fasc. 2 to *Kerygma und Dogma*

(Göttingen: Vandenhoeck & Ruprecht, 1971); "Katholizität," in K. Raiser, ed., *Löwen 1971: Studienberichte und Dokumente der Kommission für Glauben und Kirchenverfassung, Ökumenische Rundschau* 18/19 (Stuttgart: Evang. Missionsverlag, 1971), 136–61.

2. See K. Lehmann and W. Pannenberg, eds., *Lehrverurteilungen, kirchentrennend?* (Freiburg: Herder; Göttingen: Vandenhoeck & Ruprecht, 1986), 1:161; Eng. trans.: K. Lehmann and W. Pannenberg, eds., *The Condemnations of the Reformation Era: Do They Still Divide?* trans. Margaret Kohl (Minneapolis: Fortress Press, 1990).

3. See ibid., 167.

4. See ibid., 167–69.

5. "Die Kirche in Gottes Heilsplan," quoted in *Die Einheit der Kirche: Material der ökumenischen Bewegung*, Theologische Bücherei 30, ed. L. Vischer (Munich: Kaiser, 1965), 84f.

6. *Taufe, Eucharistie und Amt: Konvergenzerklärungen der Kommission für Glauben und Kirchenverfassung des Ökumenischen Rates der Kirchen* (Frankfurt and Paderborn, 1982), 44 (Ministry no. 38), quoted in Lehmann and Pannenberg, eds., *Lehrverurteilungen, kirchentrennend?* 1:165. See also *Das geistliche Amt in der Kirche* (Paderborn: Bonifatius-Druckerei; Frankfurt: O. Lembeck, 1981), 42ff.; *Einheit vor uns* (Paderborn: Bonifatius-Druckerei; Frankfurt: O. Lembeck, 1985), 60ff.

7. *Kirchengemeinschaft in Wort und Sakrament* (Paderborn: Bonifatius; Hannover: Lutherisches Verlagshaus, 1984), 14. On the question of the apostolic succession, see 79ff.

8. See the brief note in Lehmann and Pannenberg, eds., *Lehrverurteilungen, kirchentrennend?* 1:28, which unfortunately is not taken up in later discussions, although it is stated that the question of the church's mediation of salvation is still problematic

(1:63). The unresolved questions about the sacrament of penance show how important the ecclesiological issue remains. It was not by chance that the Reformation was ignited by controversies about this sacrament, and we are surely justified in seeing agreement on penance as a touchstone of consensus on the doctrine of justification (see 1:65).

9. See the overview by E. M. Kredel, "Der Apostelbegriff in der neueren Exegese," *Zeitschrift für katholische Theologie* 78 (1956): 169–93, 257–305; R. Schnackenburg, "L'apostolicité: Etat de la recherche," *Istina* 14 (1969): 5–32; J. Roloff, "Apostel/Apostolat/Apostolizität," *Theologisches Realenzyklopädie* 3:430–45.

10. G. Söhngen, "Überlieferung und apostolische Verkündigung," in idem, *Die Einheit in der Theologie: Gesammelte Abhandlungen, Aufsätze, Vorträge* (Munich: K. Zink, 1952), 317. Karl Rahner argues in a similar manner with regard to the earliest church as a whole and to Scripture: *Über die Schriftinspiration,* Quaestiones Disputatae 1 (Freiburg: Herder, 1958), 50–58; Eng. trans.: *Inspiration in the Bible* (New York: Herder and Herder, 1961).

11. See *STh* III 60,3.

12. The eschatological character is emphasized strongly by W. Pannenberg, "Apostolizität und Katholizität der Kirche in der Perspektive der Eschatologie," *Theologische Literaturzeitung* 94 (1969): 97–112, and is linked to a pneumatological conception of the church as *communio* by J. D. Zizioulas, "Apostolic Continuity and Succession," in idem, *Being as Communion: Studies in Personhood and the Church* (Crestwood, N.Y. : St. Vladimir's Seminary Press, 1985), 171–208.

13. See Y. Congar, "Le Saint-Esprit et le Corps apostolique, réalisateurs de l'oeuvre du Christ," in idem, *Esquisses du Mystère*

de l'Eglise, 2d ed., Unam Sanctam 8 (Paris: Éditions du Cerf, 1953), 129–79.

14. See W. Breuning, "Successio apostolica," *Lexikon für Theologie und Kirche*, 2d ed., 9:1143.

15. A typical proponent of this view, against the background of a Romantic-Idealistic vision, was J. S. Drey, *Die Apologetik als wissenschaftliche Nachweisung der Göttlichkeit des Christentums in seiner Erscheinung*, 2d ed. (Mainz: Florian Kupferberg, 1844), 357, 372–78. This primarily "vertical" understanding of the apostolic succession is maintained in another terminology, this time strictly Thomistic, by C. Journet, who offers the following definition: "Accordingly, apostolicity means the supernatural virtue (formal aspect) which, in order to form the church (final cause) among human beings (material cause), descends from God (efficient first cause) and then from Christ (instrumental cause joined to the divinity), then from an apostolic body conserved in existence by an uninterrupted succession (instrumental cause separated from the divinity)": *L'Eglise du Verbe incarné: Essai de théologie spéculative*, 2d ed. (Paris, 1955), 1:680; Eng. trans.: *The Church of the Word Incarnate* (London and New York: Sheed and Ward, 1955). Journet adds: "Although the hierarchical or apostolic powers are transmitted by visible rites that can leave their mark on the sands of history, they remain nonetheless intrinsically exempt from historical, rational, or psychological investigation.... We believe in apostolicity just as we believe in the church: *credo...apostolicam Ecclesiam*" (1:683). I too maintain this view in principle, though with the difference that the church and its apostolicity will be considered not only in a christological-incarnational perspective, but also in a pneumatological perspective.

16. See the bibliography in G. Blum, "Apostel/Apostolat/ Apostolizität II," *Theologisches Realenzyklopädie* 3:465f. I have found the following studies by Yves Congar particularly useful: "Composantes et idée de la Succession Apostolique," *Œcumenica* I (1966): 61–80; "Apostolicité de ministère et apostolicité de doctrine," in *Volk Gottes: Zum Kirchenverständnis der katholischen, evangelischen und anglikanischen Theologie*, Festschrift for J. Höfer, ed. R. Bäumer and H. Dolch (Freiburg: Herder, 1967), 84–111, quoted from reprint in Congar, *Ministères et communion ecclésiale* (Paris: Éditions du Cerf, 1971), 51–94.

17. Preface to the third book of *Adversus Haereses*.

18. *Adversus Haereses* 3.1.1.

19. Ibid., 3.4.2; see also 3.24.1.

20. Ibid., 3.2.2; 3.3.1; 4.26.5.

21. Ibid., 3.3.3; see also 3.4.1.

22. Ibid., 4.26.2.

23. Ibid., 4.33.8.

24. See Congar, "Composantes," 67.

25. See J. Ratzinger, "Primat, Episkopat und successio apostolica," in *Episkopat und Primat*, ed. K. Rahner and J. Ratzinger, Quaestiones Disputatae 11 (Freiburg: Herder, 1961), 49; Eng. trans.: *The Episcopate and the Primacy* (Freiburg: Herder; Montreal: Palm, 1962). Congar argues similarly, "Composantes," 63ff.

26. This is prescribed by canon 4 of the Council of Nicaea (325).

27. See B. Botte, "Der Kollegialcharakter des Priester- und Bischofsamtes," in *Das apostolische Amt*, ed. J. Gneyst (Mainz: Grünewald, 1961), 68–91; J. Colson, *L'épiscopat catholique: Collégialité et primauté dans les trois premiers siècles de l'Église* (Paris: Éditions du Cerf, 1963).

28. *De unitate ecclesiae* 4.

29. *De Baptismo* 4.31.

30. Tertullian, *Praescr.* 32. See Congar, "Composantes."

31. See Ratzinger, *Theologische Prinzipienlehre* (n. 1 above), 256.

32. This observation is fundamental for ecumenical dialogue about the apostolic succession. See the Declaration of the ecumenical committee of the united Protestant church in Germany on the question of apostolic succession: *Evangelisch-lutherische Kirchenzeitung* 12 (1958): 72–74.

33. *Adversus Haereses* 4.26.2.

34. *De unitate ecclesiae* 11.28.

35. See Congar, "Composantes," 69ff.; on the passages in Thomas, see 78f. The most interesting text is *Ver.* 14.10 ad 11: "We believe the successors of the apostles and the prophets only to the extent that they proclaim to us what the apostles and the prophets have bequeathed to us in Scripture."

36. See H. Küng, *Strukturen der Kirche,* Quaestiones Disputatae 17 (Freiburg: Herder, 1962), 228–44; Eng. trans.: *Structures of the Church* (New York: Crossroad, 1962, 1982).

37. See J. H. Newman, *On Consulting the Faithful in Matters of Doctrine,* first published in *The Rambler* (July 1859).

38. *Lumen Gentium* 8 and 15; *Unitatis Redintegratio* 2f. The dialectic of Augustine's ecclesiology — where many outside are really inside, while many inside are really outside (*De Baptismo* 5.28.39, et al.) — did not lead to the acknowledgment of the working and fruitfulness of the Spirit outside the Catholic Church (ibid., 1.1.2; 4.17.24, et al.), but he did prepare the ground for the later development with his emphatic insistence, in debate with the Donatists, that the true subject of the church's actions is Christ himself (*In Ioannem* 5.18; 6.7f.; 15.3; *De Baptismo*

3.10, et al.). See. F. Hofmann, *Der Kirchenbegriff des hl. Augustinus* (Munich: Max Hueber, 1933), 221–56; Y. Congar, "Die Lehre von der Kirche: Von Augustinus bis zum Abendländischen Schisma," *Handbuch der Dogmengeschichte* 3/3c:3–6.

39. *STh* III 64.7.

40. The fundamental study of this issue remains H. de Lubac, *Corpus Mysticum: l'eucharistie et l'église au Moyen Âge, Étude historique*, 2d ed. (Paris: Aubier, 1949).

41. See Congar, "Die Lehre von der Kirche," 96, 100f.

42. See H. Ott, "Das Weihesakrament," *Handbuch der Dogmengeschichte* 4/5:80–87.

43. See W. Kasper, "Zur Frage der Anerkennung der Ämter in den lutherischen Kirchen," *Theologische Quartalschrift* 151 (1971): 99–104. That essay is not primarily concerned with presbyteral succession; the reference to these papal jurisdictional acts was intended to show that the question of recognition of ministries demands a properly spiritual judgment. The present essay seeks to present the same concern in a wider context and to specify in greater detail what it entails.

44. This is the view correctly maintained by H. Fries and K. Rahner, *Einigung der Kirchen — reale Möglichkeit*, Questiones Disputatae 100 (Freiburg: Herder, 1983), 117; Eng. trans.: *Unity of the Churches — An Actual Possibility* (Philadelphia: Fortress Press; New York: Paulist Press, 1985).

45. See the brief summary in *Das geistliche Amt in der Kirche*, esp. 27ff.; *Kirchengemeinschaft in Wort und Sakrament*, 65ff.; Lehmann and Pannenberg, eds., *Lehrverurteilungen, kirchentrennend?* 1:157ff.

46. See Confessio Augustana 28.20ff. (Bekenntnisschriften der evangelisch-lutherischen Kirche [BSLK] 123f.); Apology for

Confessio Augustana 14; 28.6–8 (BSLK 296f., 398f.); Schmalkaldic Articles 2.4; 3.10 (BSLK 430, 457f.); *De potestate et primatu papae* 12–18, 60–73 (BSLK 474ff., 489ff.); Formula of Concord *Solida Declaratio* 10 (BSLK 1060). See *Das geistliche Amt in der Kirche*, 44f.; *Einheit vor uns*, 60f.; *Kirchengemeinschaft in Wort und Sakrament*, 80f.; Lehmann and Pannenberg, eds., *Lehrverurteilungen, kirchentrennend?* 1:162–65.

47. See Luther's affirmations about the *successio fidelium* (WA (Luther, Kritische Gesamtausgabe ("Weimar" edition) 3:169; 4:165) and his pamphlet "That a Christian Assembly or Community Has the Right and Power to Judge All Doctrine and to Call, Install and Depose Teachers: Scriptural Proofs," WA 11:408–16. The expression *successio fidelium* is also found in Thomas Aquinas: *STh* III 25.3 ad 4.

48. See Apology for Confessio Augustana 7.22 (BSLK 238f.); Calvin, *Institutes* 4.2.3.

49. See WA 39.I.191.28: *Haec est vera definitio Ecclesiae, non quae succedit Apostolis, sed quae confitetur, quod Christus sit filius Dei.* 39.II.176.5; 177.1: *Successio ad Evangelium est alligata....* We must see where the *verbum* is... *Ubi est verbum, ibi est Ecclesia... Credendum est episcopo, non quia succedit episcopo hujus loci, sed quia docet Evangelium.* The *Evangelium* is to be the *successio.* See Melanchthon, *De ecclesia et de auctoritate verbi Dei: Haec verba gravissime monent nos, ne de Ecclesia cogitemus, tanquam de mundana politia, ne eam successione Episcoporum, aut gradu et loco Pontificum metiamur, sed apud eos esse statuamus Ecclesiam, qui retinent veram doctrinam Evangelii* (Corpus Reformatorum 23.597f.); Calvin, *Institutes* 4.2.2: "To speak of [episcopal] succession counts for nothing, if the successors do not... preserve the truth of Christ inviolate and incorrupt, and abide in this truth"; 4.2.4: the distinguishing mark of the church is the Word of God.

"Wherever one can see this mark, it cannot deceive, but points with certainty to the place where the church is. Where, however, this mark is missing, nothing remains to give a genuine indicator of the church." See also the resolute affirmations by Karl Barth, *Kirchliche Dogmatik* IV/1:798–805.

50. "Katholizität und Apostolizität," *Löwen 1971*, 150f.; *Kirchengemeinschaft in Wort und Sakrament*, 81–83; *Taufe, Eucharistie und Amt*, 44; Lehmann and Pannenberg, eds., *Lehrverurteilungen, kirchentrennend?* 1:165.

51. See Apology for Confessio Augustana 7.20 (BSLK 238).

52. See Confessio Augustana 5 (BSLK 58); Heidelberg catechism, questions 65f.; Calvin, *Institutes* 4.1.1, 5f.; 2.1; 8.13.

53. See Lehmann and Pannenberg, eds., *Lehrverurteilungen, kirchentrennend?* 1:63.

54. This is also argued by Congar: "Apostolicité," 90f.; "Composantes," 70f.; *La tradition et les traditions* 1 (Paris: A. Fayard, 1960), 186f.; 2 (Paris: A. Fayard, 1963), 220–23; Eng. trans.: *Tradition and Traditions: An Historical and a Theological Essay* (London: Burns & Oates, 1966).

55. F. Schleiermacher, *Der christliche Glaube*, ed. M. Recker (Berlin: de Gruyter, 1960), §24, 137; Eng. trans.: *The Christian Faith* (Edinburgh: T. & T. Clark, 1999).

56. On the teaching of the Council of Trent about the sacrament of orders, see H. Ott, "Das Weihesakrament," 119–27; K. Becker, *Der priesterliche Dienst*, 2: *Wesen und Vollmachten des Priestertums nach dem Lehramt*, Quaestiones Disputatae 47 (Freiburg: Herder, 1970), 92–109.

57. Denziger-Hünnerman, 1501, 1507.

58. Ibid., 1768.

59. See Congar, "Apostolicité," 82f.; *La tradition*, 1:223, 233f.

60. DH 1777; see also 1769.
61. Ibid., 1769.
62. On this, see Kasper, "Zur Frage der Anerkennung" (n. 43 above), 102–4. For a critique of the isolated emphasis on the category of "validity," and a suggestion how this can be widened and deepened where the church is understood as the "rootsacrament," see A. Müller, "Amt als Kriterium der Kirchlichkeit? Kirchlichkeit als Kriterium des Amtes?" in *Kirche und Sakrament*, Theologische Berichte (Zurich: Benziger, 1980), 116–28.
63. *Lumen Gentium* 1, 9, 48, 59, etc.; see W. Beinert, "Die Sakramentalität der Kirche im theologischen Gespräch," in *Kirche und Sakrament* Theologische Berichte (Zurich: Benziger, 1980), 13–66; W. Kasper, "Die Kirche als universales Sakrament des Heils," in *Glaube im Prozeß*, ed. E. Klinger and K. Wittstadt, Festschrift for K. Rahner (Herder: Freiburg, 1984), 221–39.
64. See W. Beinert in *Glaube im Prozeß*, 44–50; *Die Sakramentalität der Kirche in der ökumenischen Diskussion*, ed. Johann-Adam-Möhler-Institut, Konfessionskundliche Schriften 15 (Paderborn: Bonifatius-Druckerei, 1983), esp. the essay by G. Gassmann, 171–201; E. Jüngel, "Kirche als Sakrament?" *Zeitschrift für Theologie und Kirche* 80 (1983): 432–57 (on the polarity between the Word of God and the church, see 451f.).
65. *Lumen Gentium* 21.
66. Ibid., 20.
67. *Dei Verbum* 8f.
68. *Ad Gentes* 3–5.
69. Ibid., 4.
70. *Lumen Gentium* 20.
71. Ibid., 28. See the commentary by A. Grillmeier, *Lexikon für Theologie und Kirche*, supplementary volume, 1:248f.

72. See the commentary by K. Rahner, ibid., 221; Kasper, "Zur Frage der Anerkennung" (n. 43 above), 103 n. 31.

73. *Unitatis Redintegratio* 22.

74. *Lumen Gentium* 8.

75. *Unitatis Redintegratio* 3.

76. See J. Hamer, "Die ekklesiologische Terminologie des Vatikanum II und die protestantischen Ämter," *Catholica* 26 (Munich, 1972), 153.

77. *Unitatis Redintegratio* 15.

78. See *Das geistliche Amt in der Kirche*, 51.

79. *Dei Verbum* 9.

80. Ibid., 10. See the commentary by J. Ratzinger, *LThK.E* 2:520: "There is virtually no trace of any element critical of the tradition." He makes similar observations on pp. 522f. and 528 with reference to *Dei Verbum* 21: "*De facto*, Scripture is given the role of criterion here." Finally, however, we note this observation: "A strict polarity between Scripture and church...is...*a priori* impossible; it is ultimately impossible to understand Scripture and church as antithetical" (525).

81. See Lehmann and Pannenberg, eds., *Lehrverurteilungen, kirchentrennend?* 1:31, although the formulations are not particularly clear: an *interpretatio benevola* of Vatican II leads to the affirmation that there "already exists an implicit consensus on many points" (30), but we also read that "there is not yet any explicit consensus" (33). I shall indicate in the next section of this essay how we might make progress on this decisive question.

82. This is argued in detail in *Einheit vor uns*, 53ff.

83. On this, see ibid., 24; O. Cullmann, *Einheit durch Vielfalt: Grundlegung und Beitrag zur Diskussion über die Möglichkeit ihrer Verwirklichung* (Tübingen: Mohr, 1986); Eng. trans.: *Unity through*

Diversity: Its Foundation, and a Contribution to the Discussion concerning the Possibilities of Its Actualization (Philadelphia: Fortress Press, 1988). Cullmann, however, discusses the problem of unity onesidedly as the problem of a superstructure, not in a sacramental perspective.

84. *Unitatis Redintegratio* 4.

85. See K. Rahner and H. Vorgrimler, "Successio apostolica," *Kleines theologisches Wörterbuch*, 10th ed. (Freiburg: Herder, 1976), 395; in English see *Dictionary of Theology*, 2d ed. (New York: Crossroad, 1981).

86. See Zizioulas, "Apostolic Continuity and Succession," in *Being as Communion*, 171–208.

87. Ibid., 207.

88. Orthodox theologians do not agree whether such an acknowledgment "in accordance with *oikonomia*" is possible. See Congar, "Composantes," 64; J. D. Zizioulas, "Ministry and Communion," in *Being as Communion*, 245f. Catholic theology sometimes attempts to take a comparable path with the help of the principle *supplet ecclesia*. See Kasper, "Zur Frage der Anerkennung" (n. 43 above), 107, n. 46. If this principle is given a new and deeper foundation in the idea of the church as "root-sacrament," it can prove helpful in the question of recognition of ministries. See Müller, "Amt als Kriterium der Kirchlichkeit?" 123ff.

89. In the case of the doctrine of primacy, J. Ratzinger has shown the extent to which an agreement with the Eastern churches is possible on the basis of the first millennium: see *Theologische Prinzipienlehre* (n. 21 above), 209.

90. On the renewal of ecclesiology from a pneumatological perspective, see W. Kasper, "Die Kirche als Sakrament des

Geistes," in idem and G. Sauter, *Kirche: Ort des Geistes* (Freiburg: Herder, 1976), 13–55; Y. Congar, *Der Heilige Geist,* 2d ed. (Freiburg: Herder, 1986), 157–212, esp. 190–200: "Der Heilige Geist erhält die Kirche in der 'Apostolizität'"; in English see Congar, *I Believe in the Holy Spirit* (New York: Seabury, 1983).

Chapter 5: Canon Law

1. See G. Quell, art. Δικη, *Theologische Wörterbuch zum Neuen Testament (TWNT)* 2:176ff.; in English see *Theological Dictionary of the New Testament.*

2. Ps. 7:9; 9:9, etc.; Isa. 11:4; Jer. 12:1, etc.

3. On what follows, see R. Bultmann, art. ἔλεος, *TWNT* 2:474ff.

4. Exod. 20:6; 34:6; Num. 14:18; Deut. 4:31; 7:9, etc.

5. Luke 1:54, 58, 72, 78, etc.

6. Matt. 9:13; 12:7 with reference to Hos. 6:6; Eph. 4:32; Col. 3:12, etc.

7. See John Paul II, encyclical *Dives in Misericordia* 3.

8. Commentary on Matt. 5:7, in A. Guarienti, ed., *Catena Aurea* (Turin and Rome, 1953), 1:74.

9. *STh* I 21,3 ad 2.

10. *STh* II-II 30,4.

11. *Dives in misericordia* 14.

12. *Lumen Gentium* 1, etc.

13. Ibid., 8.

14. See T. Schüller, *Die Barmherzigkeit als Prinzip der Rechtsapplikation in der Kirche im Dienste der salus animarum: Ein kanonistischer Beitrag zu Methodenproblemen der Kirchenrechtstheorie* (Würzburg: Echter, 1993), 293ff.

15. *Quodlibetalia* 12,16,2 (Turin and Rome, 1949), 249.

16. CIC (*Codex Iuris Canonici,* Code of Canon Law) (1983), canon 1752.
17. See Schüller, *Die Barmherzigkeit,* 317f.
18. See H. Müller, "Barmherzigkeit in der Rechtsordnung der Kirche?" *Archiv für katholisches Kirchenrecht* 159 (1990): 358ff.; Schüller, *Die Barmherzigkeit,* 321ff.
19. *Nicomachean Ethics* 5:14 (1137B–1138A).
20. Quoted by Müller, "Barmherzigkeit in der Rechtsordnung der Kirche?" 362, n. 64; Schüller, *Die Barmherzigkeit,* 357.
21. On this, see G. Virt, *Epikie, verantwortlicher Umgang mit Normen: Eine historisch-systematische Untersuchung zu Aristoteles, Thomas von Aquin und Franz Suarez* (Mainz: Matthias-Grünewald, 1983).
22. *STh* II-II 120.
23. See Virt, *Epikie,* 164ff.
24. Ibid., 171.
25. See Schüller, *Die Barmherzigkeit,* 382ff.
26. *CIC* (1983), xxxix, xli.
27. See T. Mayer-Maly, "Recht," *Staatslexikon im Auftrag der Görres-Gesellschaft unter Mitwirkung zahlreicher Fachleute,* 7th ed., 4: 678–82; Schüller, *Die Barmherzigkeit,* 264ff., esp. 280ff.
28. On the virtue of prudence, see J. Pieper, *Das Viergespann: Klugheit, Gerechtigkeit, Tapferkeit, Mut* (Munich: Kösel, 1964), 13–64; Eng. trans.: *The Four Cardinal Virtues: Prudence, Justice, Fortitude, Temperance* (Notre Dame, Ind.: University of Notre Dame Press, 1966).
29. These are more numerous than in the 1917 code: see the list in Schüller, *Die Barmherzigkeit,* 393f.
30. A. Hollerbach, "Billigkeit," *StL,* 7th ed., 1:812–13.
31. On this spiritual view, see H. Mussinghoff, "Nobile est munus ius dicere iustitiam adhibens aequitate coniunctam," in

Theologia et ius canonicum, ed. H. J. F. Reinhardt, Festschrift for H. Heinemann (Essen: Ludgerus, 1995), 21–37.

Chapter 6: The Universal Church and the Local Church

1. See "Zur Theologie und Praxis des bischöflichen Amtes," in *Auf neue Art Kirche sein,* W. Schreer and G. Steins, Festschrift for J. Homeyer (Munich: Don Bosco Verlag, 1999), 32–48.

2. "Ecclesiologia della Costituzione 'Lumen gentium,'" in *Il Concilio Vaticano II: Recezione e attualità alla luce del Giubileo,* ed. R. Fisichella (Cisinello Balsamo [Milan]: San Paolo, 2000), 66–81.

3. J. Ratzinger has convincingly presented the double ministry of unity and shown how the bishop is the link between the ministry of unity in his local church and that in the universal church: Ratzinger, *Zur Gemeinschaft gerufen: Kirche heute verstehen* (Herder: Freiburg, 1991), 89f.

4. *Lumen Gentium* 27, 37; *Christus Dominus* 16.

5. *Lumen Gentium* 26; *Christus Dominus* 11.

6. *Lumen Gentium* 27.

7. *Christus Dominus* 8.

8. Archbishop John R. Quinn's Oxford lecture attracted wide attention; see "The Claims of the Primacy and the Costly Call to Unity," in *The Exercise of the Primacy,* ed. P. Zagano and T. W. Tilley (New York: Crossroad, 1997). Cardinal Franz König and Cardinal Carlo Maria Martini are only two of many who have made similar observations.

9. "Letter to the Bishops of the Catholic Church on Some Aspects of the Church Understood as Communion" (May 18, 1992), 9 (italics in the official English text published by the Vatican).

10. See for example my essay "Kirche als communio," in Kasper, *Theologie und Kirche* (Mainz: Matthias-Grünewald, 1987), 1:272–89. Cardinal Ratzinger is right to criticize a purely horizontal understanding of *communio*. I cannot, however, for the life of me detect any trace of such a view in this text.

11. J. Gnilka, *Theologie des Neuen Testaments* (Freiburg: Herder, 1994), 10.

12. Ibid., 334.

13. Ibid., 218, 224.

14. Ignatius of Antioch, inscription to the Ephesians and other letters. Other testimonies can be found in H. de Lubac, *Quellen kirchlicher Einheit* (Einsiedeln: Johannes, 1974), 49.

15. L. Hertling was the first to present a thorough analysis of the patristic ecclesiology of *communio*. See "Communio und Primat: Kirche und Papsttum in der Antike," *Una Sancta* 17 (1962): 91–125. This interpretation has been confirmed and developed by many other scholars. See the important contributions by J. Ratzinger: *Das neue Volk Gottes: Entwürfe zur Ekklesiologie* (Düsseldorf: Patmos, 1969); *Zur Gemeinschaft gerufen* (n. 3 above), 70–88.

16. See canon 4 of the Council of Nicaea (325).

17. See canons 4, 6, 8.

18. K. Baus in *Handbuch der Kirchengeschichte* (Freiburg: Herder, 1973), II/1:38–42; Eng. trans.: Hubert Jedin and John Dolan, eds., *Handbook of Church History* (New York: Herder and Herder, 1965–81); G. Schwaiger, *Päpstlicher Primat und Autorität der Allgemeinen Konzilien im Spiegel der Geschichte* (Munich: Paderborn, 1977), 27.

19. *Romans*, inscr.

20. On this interpretation, see Schwaiger, *Päpstlicher Primat und Autorität*, 129f.

21. This lecture was reprinted without any changes after its author had been created a cardinal: J. Ratzinger, *Theologische Prinzipienlehre: Bausteine zur Fundamentaltheologie* (Munich: E. Wewel, 1982), 209. He has never retracted these words, but has later sought to defend them against misunderstandings by emphasizing that they do not mean that we should return to the first millennium, practicing an ecumenism of a "return to the past": idem, *Kirche, Ökumene, Politik* (Einsiedeln: Johannes, 1987), 76f., 81f.; Eng. trans.: *Church, Ecumenism, and Politics: New Essays in Ecclesiology* (New York: Crossroad, 1988).

22. See Y. Congar, "Die Lehre von der Kirche: Von Augustinus bis zum abendländischen Schisma," *Handbuch der Dogmengeschichte* (Freiburg: Herder, 1971), 3/3c:57f., 60f., 63f.

23. According to Congar, "Bonaventure was the most important theoretician of the papal monarchy in the thirteenth century": ibid., 144.

24. See W. Kasper, "Steuermann im Sturm: Das Bischofsamt nach Thomas von Aquin," in idem, *Theologie und Kirche* (Mainz: Matthias-Grünewald, 1999), 2:122–24.

25. Documentation and commentary by W. Kasper: *Zukunft aus der Kraft des Konzils: Die außerordentliche Bischofssynode '85* (Freiburg: Herder, 1986), 33.

26. W. Thönissen, *Gemeinschaft durch Teilhabe an Jesus Christus: Ein katholisches Modell für die Einheit der Kirchen* (Freiburg: Herder, 1996).

27. *Osservatore Romano*, June 23, 1993.

28. *Lumen Gentium* 8. On this, see the Declaration *Dominus Jesus* by the Congregation for the Doctrine of the Faith "on the

unicity and salvific universality of Jesus Christ and the church" (September 6, 2000). I cannot discuss here the problems raised by this Declaration.

29. *Lumen Gentium* 26.

30. *Lumen Gentium* 4; *Unitatis Redintegratio* 2.

31. De Lubac, *Quellen kirchlicher Einheit*, 50.

32. Letter of the Congregation, 9 (italics original).

33. M. Theobald, "Der römische Zentralismus und die Jerusalemer Urgemeinde," *Theologische Quartalschrift* 180 (2000): 225–28.

34. 2 Clement 14.2; Hermas, *Shepherd, Vis.* 2.4. On Origen, see P.-T. Camelot, "Die Lehre von der Kirche: Väterzeit bis ausschließlich Augustinus," in *Handbuch der Dogmengeschichte* (Freiburg: Herder, 1970), 3/3b:9; on Augustine, see Congar, "Die Lehre von der Kirche" (n. 22 above), 6–8.

35. See art. "Präexistenzvorstellungen," *Lexikon für Theologie und Kirche*, 3d ed. 8:491–93.

36. See H. de Lubac, *Quellen kirchlicher Einheit* (n. 14 above), 52f. De Lubac is an unimpeachable witness here, since he warns explicitly in another passage against the dangers of a sociological perspective and an exaggerated nationalism. Nevertheless, he makes it clear that the sociocultural factor has considerable significance for the evaluation of this question (see 45f.).

37. The medieval controversy about universals dealt exhaustively with the question whether the universal exists "before," "in," or (thanks to an abstraction) only "after" the concrete.

38. J. Ratzinger, "Die Kirche und die Kirchen," *Reformatio* 13 (1964): 105.

39. See W. Kasper, "Kircheneinheit und Kirchengemeinschaft in katholischer Perspektive: Eine Problemskizze," *Glaube und*

Gemeinschaft, Festschrift for P. W. Scheele (Würzburg: Echter, 2000), 100–117.
40. *Unitatis Redintegratio* 4.
41. DH 3961; *Lumen Gentium* 27.
42. *Ut unum sint* 95.

The First Publication of the Essays

Chapter 1: "Der Diakon in ekklesiologischer Sicht angesichts der gegenwärtigen Herausforderungen in Kirche und Gesellschaft," *Diakonia* 32, nos. 3–4 (1997), 13–33; also in W. Kasper, *Theologie und Kirche* (Mainz: Matthias-Grünewald, 1999), 2:145–62.

Chapter 2: "Der priesterlicher Dienst: Repräsentation Jesu Christi als Haupt der Kirche," in W. Kasper, *Nicht Herren eures Glaubens, sondern Diener eurer Freude: Gedanken zum priestlichen Dienst anläßlich des 40jährigen Priesterjubiläums am 6. April 1997* (Rottenburg: Bischöflichen Ordinariat der Diözese Rottenburg-Stuttgart, 1997), 16–32; also in W. Kasper, *Theologie und Kirche* (Mainz: Matthias-Grünewald, 1999), 2:128–44.

Chapter 3: "Steuermann mitten im Sturm: Das Bischofsamt nach Thomas von Aquin," in W. Kasper, *Theologie und Kirche* (Mainz: Matthias-Grünewald-Verlag, 1987, 1999), 2:103–27.

Chapter 4: "Die apostolische Sukzession als ökumenisches Problem," in *Lehrverurteilungen, kirchentrennend?* ed. W. Pannenberg (Freiburg: Herder; Göttingen: Vandenhoeck & Ruprecht, 1990), 3:329–49; also in W. Kasper, *Theologie und Kirche* (Mainz: Matthias-Grünewald, 1999), 2:163–82.

Chapter 5: "Gerechtigkeit und Barmherzigkeit: Überlegungen zu einer Applikationstheorie kirchenrechtlicher Normen," in *Iustitia in*

Caritate, ed. R. Puza and A. Weiß, Festschrift for E. Rößler (Frankfurt and New York: P. Lang, 1997), 59–66; also in W. Kasper, *Theologie und Kirche* (Mainz: Matthias-Grünewald, 1999), 2:183–91. The translation of chapters 2–5 follows where appropriate the revised version in W. Kasper, *Theologie und Kirche* 2 (Mainz: Matthias-Grünewald-Verlag, 1999).

Chapter 6: "Das Verhältnis von Universalkirche und Ortskirche: Freundschaftliche Auseinandersetzung mit der Kritik von Joseph Kardinal Ratzinger," *Stimmen der Zeit* 219 (December 2000): 795–804.

Chapter 7: "Ein Herr, ein Glaube, eine Taufe: Ökumenische Perspektiven für die Zukunft," *Stimmen der Zeit* 220 (February 2002): 75–89.